Praise for *Women Waking Up*

"*Women Waking Up* is a must-read for any woman who reaches midlife seeking transformation and yearning for more freedom. Wendy Valentine guides her readers in creating a new vision for their lives and shows them step-by-step how to get there."

— **Kristine Carlson**, coauthor of the *Don't Sweat the Small Stuff* series

"*Women Waking Up* is the perfect guide for transforming midlife crisis into midlife awakening. Find your power again by following Wendy Valentine's seven-step process to reclaim your vitality, joy, and healing."

— **HeatherAsh Amara**, author of *Warrior Goddess Training* and *Wild, Willing, and Wise*

"*Women Waking Up* is a rallying cry for anyone who has ever felt their light dim under the weight of life's responsibilities. This book is a powerful guide to reigniting your inner strength, rediscovering your unique gifts, and stepping into the second half of life with boldness and purpose. The message is clear: Your superhero has been there all along — waiting for you to wake her up and unleash her full potential. If you're ready to swap exhaustion for excitement and hesitation for heroism, this book is your roadmap. It's time to put on your cape and take the world by storm!"

— **Jenn Drummond**, world record–holding mountaineer, speaker, and author of *BreakProof*

"What an inspiration Wendy Valentine is! Any conversation with her leaves you uplifted and empowered. She is lighting the way for women who are ready for more in their lives: more vitality, more engagement, more joy, more authentic living. Her real-life, living example shows how, when you put your mind to it, you can step into what you have always known in your heart was out there waiting for you. Dig in and enjoy her book — be inspired for more!"

— **Kate Wells**, MBA, CEO of Parlor Games

"*Women Waking Up* is the book I wish every woman could read as she enters midlife. It's honest, empowering, and deeply relatable — a roadmap to turning life's challenges into opportunities for growth, freedom, and joy. As I read, I found myself nodding, highlighting passages, and feeling both seen and inspired. This isn't just a book; it's a wake-up call for any woman ready to step into her power and embrace midlife as her most fulfilling chapter yet."

— **Julie McFadden**, RN, *New York Times* bestselling author of *Nothing to Fear*

"I live by a golden rule: Never take advice from someone with a life I wouldn't want. When I was first introduced to Wendy Valentine, I was shocked to learn we were so close in age. I'd thought she was much younger, and I remember thinking, *I wonder why she named her podcast* The Midlife Makeover Show. Then I found out how close we were in age, and I knew right then that she was a soul sister and someone I would learn a lot from. A book like *Women Waking Up* only happens when a woman goes through hell and lives to tell her story. I'll take advice from Wendy Valentine any day of the week."

— **Paula Swope**, Chopra Certified instructor and author of *Thought SNOB*

"Wendy Valentine's *Women Waking Up* is a game changer for every woman navigating midlife with questions, doubts, or a deep desire for more. With honesty, humor, and wisdom, Wendy lays out a powerful roadmap to freedom and fulfillment. Her FREEDOM method is both practical and inspiring, giving women the tools to step into their next chapter with confidence and purpose. If you're ready to redefine midlife on your terms, this book is your guide!"

— **Stefanie Gass**, host of the *Online Business for Christian Women* podcast

"I know Wendy Valentine both professionally and personally, and I know from hearing her story that if there's anyone who knows how to navigate midlife and come out thriving, it's her! Wendy's book is absolutely amazing — filled with wisdom, humor, and a blueprint for starting your new life at midlife. If you've been hearing that silent question in your heart, *Is this all there is?* the answer is *No!* There is definitely more — all you need is Wendy's book to create your plan and Wendy as your expert guide!"

— **Camille Martin**, RD, author of
Love to Lose: Love Your Life and Watch the Weight Lose Itself

"Wendy Valentine, and her book, will ignite a spark in your soul. Her positive attitude will inspire you to take the leap you've been dreaming of. *Women Waking Up* is a call to us all to take our dreams and make them a reality."

— **Dr. Brooke Scheller**, doctor of clinical nutrition and author of
How to Eat to Change How You Drink

"*Read this book!* It's just the injection of energy you need to infuse your system with the sisterly love and *truth* that only Wendy can give you. If you're ready for your next decades to be *rocking* with juice and power, get your copy now — and get one for a girlfriend!"

— **Kim D'Eramo**, DO, bestselling author of *Be Your Own Healer*
and *The MindBody Toolkit* and founder of the
American Institute of Mind Body Medicine

"Ladies! Grab your grande latte and superhero cape — it's time for your midlife revival! Wendy Valentine's *Women Waking Up* is the ultimate guide to breaking free from what's holding you back and launching into a life that makes you want to shout *HELL YES* from the rooftops."

— **Dr. Nicole Cain**, ND, MA, author of *Panic Proof*

"Wendy Valentine has created a must-read roadmap for any woman ready to take midlife by the horns and turn it into the most vibrant chapter of her life. *Women Waking Up* is equal parts relatable, inspiring, and practical — packed with tools and stories that will make you laugh, cry, and most importantly, take action. Wendy's authentic approach makes reinvention feel not only possible but exciting. This book will empower you to step fully into the badass version of yourself that's been waiting to shine."

— **Andrea Owen**, author of *How to Stop Feeling Like Sh*t*

"This book will prove to you that you can shake up your life, wake up your heart, and start anew — and that the time to do it is now."

— **Amy B. Scher**, bestselling author of *How to Heal Yourself When No One Else Can*

"When Wendy Valentine writes a book, you need to cancel all your meetings and plans and hair appointments and sit right down with your beverage of choice (I made a margarita) and read every last page in a state of inspired rapture. It'll probably be a binge-read kind of scenario, so prepare accordingly. *Women Waking Up* is the absolute perfect prompt — from a wise and witty woman — to live a life worth living. This is a must-read for anyone looking to live like they mean it. Now go get comfy and hunker down with your reading glasses. This book is worth the read and worth buying for the women you care about."

— **Jodi Wellman**, author of *You Only Die Once: How to Make It to the End with No Regrets*

WOMEN WAKING UP

WOMEN WAKING UP

The Midlife Manifesto for Passion, Purpose, and Play

Wendy Valentine

New World Library
Novato, California

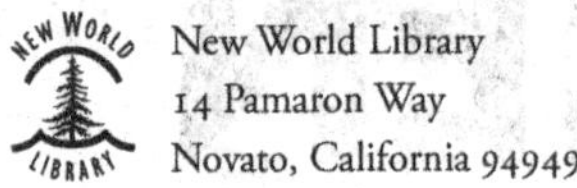

New World Library
14 Pamaron Way
Novato, California 94949

Text design by Tona Pearce Myers

Library of Congress Cataloging-in-Publication data is available.
First printing, September 2025

ISBN 978-1-60868-970-5
Ebook ISBN 978-1-60868-971-2
Printed in Canada

10 9 8 7 6 5 4 3 2

New World Library is committed to protecting our natural environment. This book is made of material from well-managed FSC®-certified forests and other controlled sources.

To Alexander, Nicholas, and Nolan:
You are my sunshine.

CONTENTS

STEP

FREE YOURSELF

1

TAKE THE WHEEL OF MIDLIFE

Have you ever had a thought or feeling about reinventing your life bubble up? Maybe it motivated you to make a change, or buy this book, or take some other risk. I applaud you for answering the call from your soul's yearning for a more fulfilling journey in life. Bravo! It's time to say *YES* to a new you. And congrats for having the insight that transformation needs to take place. The lightbulb must have gone on in your head signaling that your life needs to change — but you did the hard part, which was to pay attention to it.

This is what I call a midlife awakening, not a crisis. Midlife is a time of waking up to your true self and choosing to stay awake, present, and intentional in your life.

You might *know* you need to change, but awareness only takes you so far. Transformation takes place when you take a step forward. Not just any step, though — a step that will lead you in the right direction toward a new life — a life of joy, harmony, a ton of fun, and whatever the heck you want.

Taking that first step can be challenging. Even if you're fired up, overflowing with courage, and ready to conquer your life, you may not know which step to take first. This in itself can be overwhelming, and most people turn back before they even set foot on the path.

I can completely relate to that feeling of overwhelm and paralysis when facing change because when I hit my mid-forties, I felt like my life was crumbling around me. I was facing a mound of debt, a dried-up bank account, unemployment, divorce papers, an eerily empty nest, chronic illness, depression, anxiety, and the death of my brother. I felt completely lost, drowning in a sea of tears and hopelessness. I wanted to wave the white flag, but I was too exhausted to even lift it.

It wasn't just at this moment that everything seemed wrong. For thirty years before this, I had been struggling. Alone as a pregnant teenager, I was physically abused by my boyfriend. When my first husband died at age twenty-six, I then watched my brother abuse himself with drugs and alcohol until he put himself into a coma. I made one bad relationship choice after another, and I did everything I could to make sure everyone else was happy in my life. Except me.

I knew my life needed to change. I knew that Wendy needed to change. I had to pull myself together, wipe the mascara-streaked tears from my cheeks, and figure out a way forward. I was tired of being stuck in this awful place in my life, and I knew that something had to give. And it did.

The steps I had to take to become a happier, healthier, and more peaceful woman were delivered to me in a vision — a crazy, out-of-the-blue vision of me driving an RV across the country. That's right. Lil' me at five feet, six inches in a big RV at twenty-five feet long and twelve thousand pounds! What a wild epiphany. I'm all about receiving signs from the universe, but this one felt like something out of a dream that didn't quite make sense. Still, it was the first thought in a long time that had sparked real excitement. I decided to try this vision on for size.

At the time, I was lost in a numbing sense of despair, stuck in a life I no longer recognized or wanted. But the vision began to take shape, slowly evolving into a dream of something better. I pictured myself driving a cool, sleek motorhome into the hot desert sun, singing loudly along to Tom Cochrane's "Life Is a Highway." I imagined a new-and-improved Wendy behind the wheel — a woman with a fulfilling career, financial freedom, a healthy body, a peaceful mind, and a happy life. I could not only see myself smiling, but *feel* it. I desperately wanted more of that feeling. I wanted to feel alive again. I wanted to feel like myself.

This incredible insight brought so many wonderful feelings of hope and inspiration, and yet it also brought many scary feelings of doubt and desperation. My RV dream was quickly interrupted with a blast of questions and doubts: *How do I start a new career at the age of forty-five? How do I get rid of all this debt? How will I be healthy enough to make it happen? What makes me think I can achieve such a grand dream anyway? Look at me — I'm such a mess.*

In my hopeless and dismal state, this new vision seemed completely out of reach. I felt an overwhelming urge to give up, weighed down by the enormity of it all. But then another thought occurred to me — a quote actually. A quote that had never meant much to me until that moment.

> Two roads diverged in a wood, and I —
> I took the one less traveled by,
> And that has made all the difference.
>
> — Robert Frost, "The Road Not Taken" (1915)

That was it. I was at a crossroads in my life, and I had two choices. I could stay on the road of misery that I had traveled most of my life, or I could choose to take the road of freedom and create my future dream life. No one but I could make that choice.

Driving an RV across the country seemed really crazy, but staying stuck in the same cycle of pain and misery seemed even crazier. I realized that either road would take a ton of effort, so I might as well put my energy into building a better life for myself.

I made the choice to take the road less traveled. The road that would lead to my true, authentic self. The road that would lead to a life of freedom.

As I sat at mile zero of my journey, staring at the wreckage of my life, I began to see an opportunity to build something new. I decided if I was going to climb my way out of massive debt and recover from divorce, disease, and depression, I needed to find a way to do it myself.

Which is exactly what I did.

I opened my journal to a blank page, drew a big circle in pink pen, divided it into eight wedges, and labeled each section as one of the eight main categories of life: Family, Finance, Health, Career, Friends, Love, Leisure, and Growth. I rated each area on a scale of 1 to 10, with 1 being dissatisfied and 10 being satisfied. It came as no surprise that I ranked every category in my life under a 4. I obviously had some work to do. Next, I wrote down one simple step I could take to improve my life: *Get a job.*

I had spent the past twenty years working in the healthcare industry, mostly managing the medical practice I once shared with my husband. It wasn't work I loved — in fact, it drained me — but it helped support the family, so I stuck with it. With our divorce, that chapter ended — the job along with the marriage. I suddenly found myself unemployed, uncertain, and staring down a blank page. I craved something more meaningful, something that used my gifts. I didn't know what that dream career looked like yet, but I knew I'd need a stepping stone to get there. Any job would do, as long as it got me moving forward.

This big circle on the blank page, drawn in a moment of despair, kicked off the transformational journey that would change my life, allowing me to one day hit the open road in full freedom — and in my very own RV. And that circle became my signature tool, the Wheel of Midlife, the foundation for my proprietary process of helping women wake up and find their own new paths in their second half of life.

This was the *aha!* moment that shifted my entire life — and the road that made all the difference. This insight started a series of chain reactions that took me from broke, miserable, and crying all the time to debt-free, happy, and laughing in my brand-new motorhome. The story of how I got from point A of *angst* to point B of *bliss* — and how you can do the same — starts right here in this chapter.

Your Road to FREEDOM

Welcome to step 1 of the seven steps to FREEDOM, and welcome to the beginning of your new life. During our journey together in this book, I'll be taking you through your own midlife makeover process:

Free Yourself: I will get the wheels rolling by helping you gain clarity on where to start your journey to freedom, reactivating your strengths to uncover your purpose in life, and making your mind your best friend.

Reset Your Life: Together, we'll hit the Reset button by clearing away the clutter that holds you back and visualizing the person you want to become as you step into a fresh chapter. I'll guide you through the Lotus Effect, a subconscious release technique designed to help you rise from the muck of midlife and bloom into your fullest potential.

Envision a New Future: You'll be guided to imagine a vibrant, healthy body, an ideal lifestyle, and a future filled with purpose and joy. You'll discover practical ways to nourish and love the body that will support you through every step of your journey, along with journaling and meditation techniques to reverse-engineer your dreams into reality.

Embrace and Explore: Midlife wouldn't be very fun if you didn't explore a bit. I invite you to drop your perfectionism, embrace mistakes, try new things, and simplify the process of reinventing yourself one step at a time.

Detach from Tomorrow: It's common to worry too much about the destination and toss the joy of the journey out the window. In this step, I remind you to detach, embrace the unknown, go with the flow, and allow your triggers to become your treasures.

Own Your Badass Self: If you're going through all the effort to reinvent yourself, then you need to own who you are and the life you are creating. Learning how to set boundaries in your relationships will boost your self-esteem, self-worth, and self-acceptance to protect your newly released warrior within.

Master Yourself: I really drive it home in the final step by offering tools to help you overcome the bad days and encourage you to repeat the FREEDOM steps several times throughout your life to continually become the next best version of you.

Use this book as a guide to help you discover who you want to become, what life you want to live, and how to get there. You'll find that it is jam-packed with simple tools, thought-provoking questions, and fun practices to guide your journey. Each one is marked by a special superhero star icon — your sign that it's time to pause, reflect, and take inspired action. Keep an eye out for these little bursts of midlife magic in every chapter.

Let's get rolling with the Wheel of Midlife, a simple method to help you gain clarity and direction on where to start your journey to freedom. This is the same tool I used to go from my exhausting past to my exhilarating present.

You can't just take any step forward. You need to take a step that will lead you in the right direction toward your new life.

Let's get started!

Take the Wheel of Midlife

You may not be bumping through hundreds of miles of America in an RV like I was, but you can still gain control of your figurative wheel to take the driver's seat in your life moving forward.

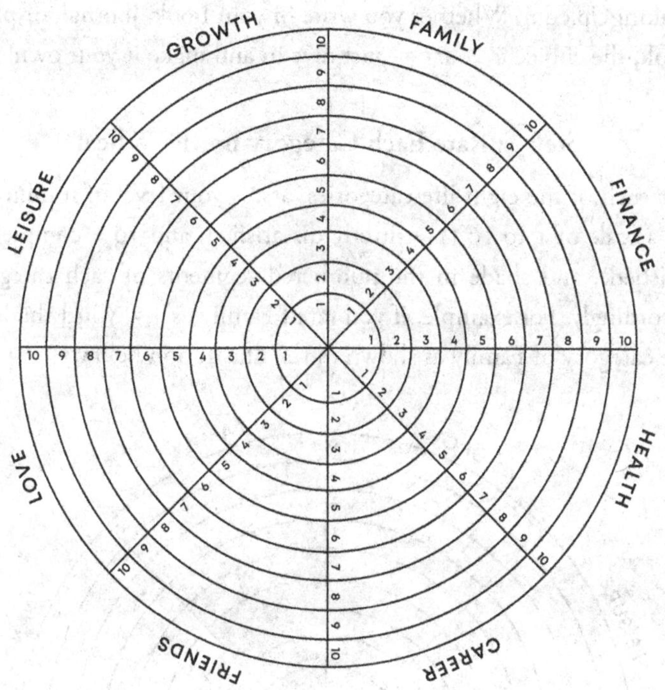

Above is the Wheel of Midlife, which contains the eight main categories of your life: Family, Finance, Health, Career, Friends, Love, Leisure, and Growth. The purpose of the Wheel of Midlife is to evaluate all areas of your life to determine which areas need the most love, attention, and transformation.

Think of each category as being a spoke on a wheel. If one of those spokes were shorter than the other spokes, it would be a rather wonky wheel. Your wheel wouldn't roll smoothly, and neither will your life. In order to have a smooth ride down the road to freedom, you need a smooth wheel. Don't worry — we will roll through this together. I'm on this road to freedom with you.

For this exercise, you can use the Wheel of Midlife provided above, draw one in your journal, or use the one available in the *Women Waking Up Playbook*, which you can download at WomenWakingUp.com. Whether you write in your book, journal, or playbook, the choice is yours — just dive in and make it your own!

Step 1: Rate Each Category on the Wheel

For each of the eight life categories, assess your level of fulfillment on a scale of 1 to 10 (1 = utterly dissatisfied, and 10 = completely satisfied), and shade in the numbered segments of each category accordingly. For example, if you rated Family as a 7, you'd shade in the category of Family as shown in the illustration below.

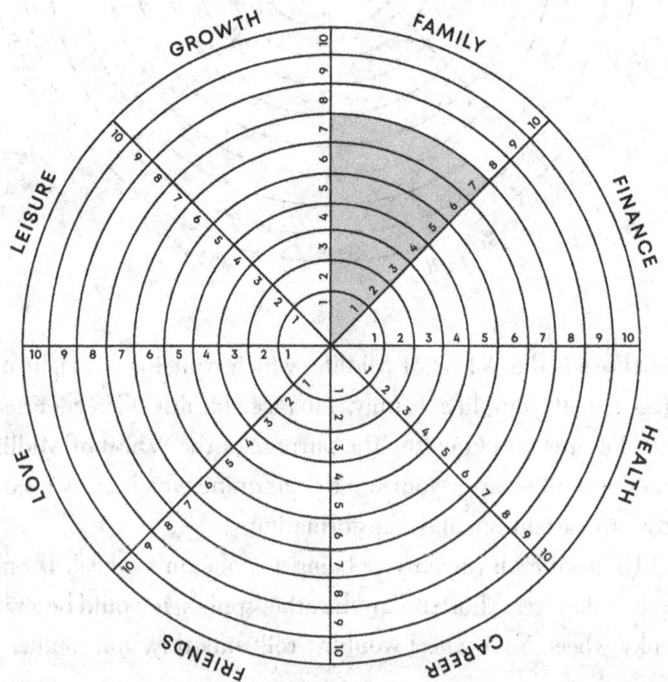

Here are some questions to ask yourself as you evaluate each category:

Family

- How would you rate the quality and amount of time you spend with your closest family members?
- What score would you assign to your relationships with the people you consider family?
- How satisfied are you with the connections and support within your family circle?

Finance

- How confident do you feel about your financial situation, both now and in the future?
- How would you evaluate the quality of your savings, investments, and pension to potentially secure your future?
- What score would you give yourself for financial independence or freedom?

Health

- How satisfied are you with your overall health, wellness, and the condition of your physical body?
- What score would you give to the quality of your eating habits and diet?
- How would you rate the quality and quantity of your sleep?

Career

- How fulfilled do you feel by your work?
- How content are you with the number of hours you work?
- To what extent are your gifts and strengths being utilized in your career?

Friends

- How satisfied are you with the number of friendships you have?
- How would you assess the depth of your friendships?
- Do you feel you have sufficient quality time with your closest friends?
- How would you rate the time you have to socialize and form new friendships and connections?

Love

- How would you evaluate the overall quality of your current intimate relationship? If you are not currently in an intimate relationship, reflect on your past relationships or your most recent one.
- What score would you give to your communication with your spouse or significant other?
- How satisfied are you with your level of romance and intimacy with your spouse or significant other?

Leisure

- How would you rate the quality of time you have each week for leisure and recreation?
- Are you satisfied with your ability to pursue your passions or hobbies?
- How would you assess the time you have for fun and laughter?

Growth

- How would you evaluate your emotional health and mental well-being?
- How aligned do you feel with an overarching vision, purpose, and direction for your life?

- What score would you give to the time you set aside for personal reflection, prayer, or meditation?

Try not to overthink the 1 to 10 scale. A 10 may mean something different to you than it means to someone else. Trust your gut.

Check out the example below of a completed Wheel of Midlife.

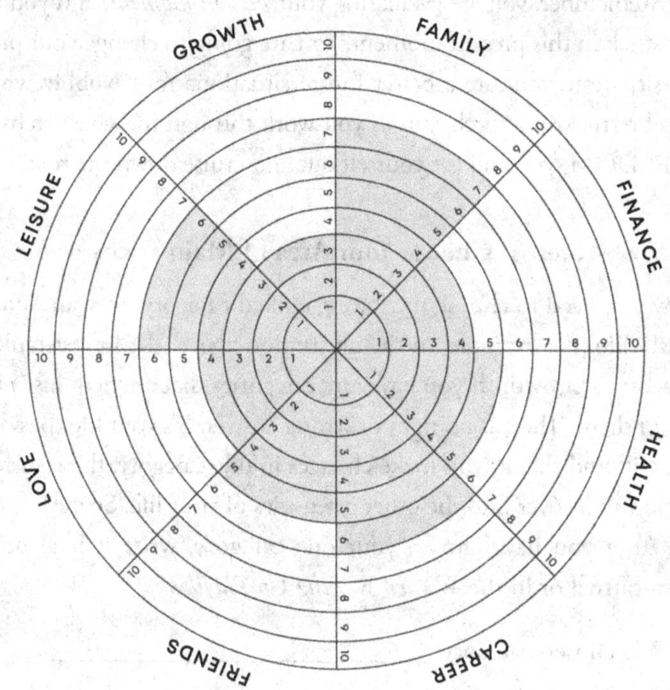

Step 2: Review Your Present Moment

Now that you have evaluated each of the eight categories in your life, sit back in your chair, take a look at your Wheel of Midlife, and answer the following questions:

- How do you feel about your life as you look at your Wheel of Midlife?
- Is there anything that surprises you? If so, what?

When I evaluated the eight categories of my life, I realized that all of them were ranked below 4. Every single one. This realization depressed me because it meant that my life was really jacked up. And it was. But I knew I had the power to change it.

You may be experiencing a similar feeling, and if you are, don't get stuck on the low numbers.

Remember, you are evaluating your *present moment*, and you are not stuck in this present moment. You are going to change your present situation to create a better future situation. Your wobbly wheel may be stuck in a ditch, but as you work through the seven steps to FREEDOM, you will get yourself out and cruise down the road.

Step 3: Choose Your Area of Main Focus

Now you need to choose the lowest-ranked category on your Wheel of Midlife. For example, in the illustration above, the lowest-ranked category is Growth. If you have any categories that are tied, just pick one of them. There is no right or wrong answer. It's your life. Besides, you will find that as you make changes in one category, the transformation spills over into the other categories of your life. Score!

After you have chosen your one category, write it here or in your journal or in the *Women Waking Up Playbook*.

My chosen category: ______________________________

This category will be your main focus during the course of this book. Boosting this category will help you balance your Wheel of Midlife, so you can invent a life you love. Let's take a more in-depth look at your chosen category.

Step 4: Dig Deeper

Now it's time to dive into your heart and dig up some answers to the following questions. Yes, there are a lot of questions, and yes you do need to answer them all if you want to reinvent your life. Trust me, it's worth it.

Answer the questions in order in your journal, and by the time you complete all of them, you will arrive at the next step in your life. Grab your pen, and let's begin.

1. Why is this category your lowest-ranked category?
2. What frustrates you the most about this area of your life?
3. How do you *currently* spend time in this area?
4. How would you *like to* spend time in this area?
5. What would a score of 10 look like to you?
6. How will it benefit you to change this area in your life?
7. How would you feel when those changes were made?
8. How could you make space for this change?
9. What help and support might you need from others to make changes and be more satisfied with this area?
10. What is your greatest fear about making this change?

Your answer to the next question is the winner, winner, chicken dinner, the one that sets everything in motion. It will lead you to take not only one step, but another step and another step and another step. This next answer is the first standing domino before you flick it with your finger and watch the other dominoes tumble on down the line. Let's reveal your big domino.

11. What is the smallest step you could take to improve this area in your life? (Just one step. No matter how tiny it is.)

Fabulous. You did it! You have laid out your first step toward your future self. Congratulations. Now let's go one step further.

Step 5: Set Your Goal

It's great to identify your first step toward improving your main area of focus, but until you pick up your foot and move forward, that first written step is only words on paper. You need to turn that step into a concrete action. And don't get overwhelmed about the whole journey — just focus on the next step. Let's make a game plan for setting goals to improve your chosen category.

Here you will learn the goal-setting method called STEP, which stands for *specifics*, *timing*, *expectations*, and *plan*. This is where you will really define and break down the *what*, *when*, and *how* of your goal.

Specifics: First, you need to set a specific goal. "I want to lose weight" is a *broad* goal. "I want to lose thirty pounds" is a *specific* goal. The more detailed you can be about your goal, the more likely you are to manifest that exact goal. Thoughts become things, so be specific in your thoughts about exactly what you want.

What is your specific goal?

Timing: Second, you need an end date to your goal — a deadline. Many of us don't like deadlines, but think of this deadline as a lifeline instead: Accomplishing this goal is your lifeline to a new life and a new you. When you set a date for accomplishing your goal, seeing that date creeping up on the calendar will encourage you to get it done. Your end date is your finish line of victory.

What is the end date for meeting your goal?

Expectations: Third, make sure you are setting a realistic expectation for yourself. "I want to lose thirty pounds by next Tuesday" is not a realistic expectation. "I want to lose thirty pounds in six months" is more realistic. If you conquer that goal in three months, then you'll really feel like a rockstar! The key is to keep it small. Conquering small goals gives a nice boost to your body, mind, and spirit. Add up all those conquered small goals, and that becomes one big boost. And sometimes a boost is all you need to keep you motivated in meeting your goals.

Is accomplishing your goal by your specified end date a realistic expectation?

Plan: Define your plan to achieve this goal. What exactly will you do every day, every week, every month to get your goal done? For example, "I will not eat ice cream at night." Notice how this is a simple, small intention with realistic expectations. "I will run five miles every morning" is unrealistic. It might be possible, but you may experience overwhelm with such a lofty plan. You want to set yourself up for success, so be kind to yourself and define simple, small actionable steps.

What action will you take to achieve this goal?

Step 6: Write Your New Goal

Now you need to put the STEP together and write your new goal.

My goal is to ________________________________
by this date: _________________. And my plan to achieve this goal is to ________________________________.

Coming Up

Yay for you! You have a goal for the first step of reinventing yourself. As you move forward in this book, you will work on achieving this goal. The upcoming chapters will provide you with more inspiration to conquer your goal and bring balance to your wheel. As I mentioned previously, when you work on improving one area of your life, the benefits will spill over into the other areas of your life. It's a win-win!

Just remember that you are not trying to reinvent yourself overnight. Rome was not built in a day, and the new you won't be either. Transformation takes time.

Now it's time to grab your cape because in the next chapter you will empower your superpower! I will walk you through a process of reactivating your natural-born badass skills through my Superhero Quiz, reconnecting you with activities that light your soul on fire.

2

EMPOWER YOUR SUPERPOWER

How long are you going to wait before you demand the best for yourself?

— Epictetus, *Discourses*

The day I sketched that wheel in my journal, the metaphorical wheel of my life was a mess. With a warped rim, bent spokes, and nail punctures, it might as well have rolled through a construction site and been run over by a truck. That image perfectly captured how I felt: deflated, broken, and teetering on the edge of collapse. Decades of navigating life's challenges — raising children, juggling multiple careers, and managing a household — had drained me of my energy and dimmed my inner light. To make matters worse, the trauma I had carried with me over the years had compounded this exhaustion, leaving me feeling as though I was barely holding it together. The superhero within me, once able to leap tall buildings in a single bound, could now barely muster the strength to get out of bed in the morning.

I realized that if I were to achieve my first goal of getting a job, courage was going to be my nonnegotiable. Without it, my wheel, which was already wobbling, wouldn't make it far. It was clear that my superpowers needed a serious jump start. Wonder Wendy had to wake up and take control of her life again.

As I began applying for jobs, I encountered something unexpected: Many potential employers required that I take personality tests, like the Myers-Briggs Type Indicator or DISC assessment. The results of these tests, designed to identify one's core strengths and preferences, were reminders of what I was naturally good at and what I genuinely enjoyed doing. This process of discovery was both eye-opening and empowering; it helped me reconnect with parts of myself that I'd thought were lost.

To my surprise, this journey of self-revelation led me to accept a job offer as a new home sales consultant for a major corporation in Chicago, Illinois — a role I had never imagined myself in, in a city I had never even visited. But deep down, I knew this job wasn't meant to be my final destination; it was a stepping stone, a means to get myself out of debt and closer to my ultimate dream of living life on the road in my very own RV. Four weeks after submitting my first job application, I packed up a moving truck and drove from Virginia to Illinois, ready to embrace my new life. It's incredible how the universe conspires to help you when you commit to moving forward — wobbly wheels and all.

Now it's your time to rise. You've read my story — now let's focus on yours. It's time to reignite your superpowers and set your wheels in motion. Let's awaken the superhero within you and start this transformative journey together.

Where's Your Superhero?

As we navigate through the first half of life, our unique gifts, talents, and strengths often get buried under the weight of everyday responsibilities. The constant grind of making a living, raising a family or managing a household, and meeting societal expectations can make it easy to lose sight of what truly makes life fulfilling — a life fueled by purpose and passion. You may have been diligently checking off all the boxes society laid out for you, appearing to have it all together on the outside, while inside you were neglecting your spirit, dimming your inner light, and gradually tucking your superhero away, as if saying, *Rest now. I'll handle this.*

All that effort you poured into building the foundation of your life may have left you feeling drained, insecure, and questioning whether you have the strength to conquer what lies ahead. It's natural to feel this way; after all, the first half of life can take a lot out of you. But this is where your superhero comes in, ready to save the day and, more importantly, your life.

Your superhero is the embodiment of your inner strength, courage, and love, and she's been waiting for the perfect moment to reemerge. She's the one who will propel you forward, slaying challenges and making the second half of your life the best it can be. And don't worry — she's still there, patiently waiting for you to tap her on the shoulder, hand her a double shot of espresso, and say, "It's time to wake up! We've got new and exciting things to do!"

Awakening your superhero, and reconnecting with her unique superpowers, is the key to unlocking your full potential. It's the moment you transition from being just another woman to being a *whoa-man*. As in, "Whoa, watch out world!" You're about to bring your A game. So go ahead, fuel up with espresso, because it's time to wake up your superhero and take the world by storm. You've got a whole new chapter to write, and it's going to be epic.

Reviving Your Superhero: A Journey to Rediscovery

After years of dedicated research, deep soul-searching, and a transformative journey that awakened my superhero, I've crafted the ultimate guide to help you experience your own revival. This chapter is designed to take you on an in-depth exploration of the Spectacular Six Superheroes — each representing a distinct aspect of your inner power. You have all six within you, but one will likely shine the brightest. You'll discover their unique superpowers, empowering superwords, powerful superstatements, energizing superboosters, depleting superdrainers, and inspiring superpursuits. And yes, it's going to be super-dee-duper!

You'll embark on a fun and revealing adventure by taking the Superhero Quiz. This quiz is designed to pinpoint which of these six superheroes mirrors your strengths, personality, and potential. Rediscovering the superhero within you isn't just a delightful exercise in self-awareness; it's about reactivating the natural-born badass skills that have been lying dormant, waiting for their moment to shine. It's about reconnecting with activities and passions that make your soul sing and light your spirit on fire.

But here's the thing: Embracing your strengths goes far beyond personal fulfillment. It's about building resilience. As you navigate the various challenges and transitions that come with midlife, your strengths act as a guiding compass. They help you steer through uncertainty, adapt to change, and thrive in the face of adversity. Rediscovering and embracing your superhero ensures that you not only survive but soar to new heights, living the vibrant, empowered life you were always meant to lead.

So get ready to fly high and harness the power within. Your superhero is ready to leap back into action, and the world is ready to be amazed by what you're capable of. Let's take this journey together and unlock your inner superpowers!

The Spectacular Six Superheroes

These six superheroes represent the diverse aspects of your character, each embodying a unique set of superpowers that you already possess. Altogether, there are eighteen superpowers, three for each of these six superheroes. While we have access to all these powers, we tend to align more closely with one superhero, reflecting the unique blend of traits that define us.

But remember, these superheroes are not just symbols or figures of inspiration; they are mirrors reflecting your own untapped potential. By understanding and embracing your primary superhero, you can harness these traits to shape a life that aligns with your deepest desires and aspirations.

Let's meet the Spectacular Six — each with their own trio of unique traits that make them truly extraordinary.

Superhero Spark: The beacon of *optimism*, *playfulness*, and *spirituality*, Spark illuminates every situation with a radiant light, encouraging us to find joy and meaning in even the smallest moments. She reminds us to embrace life with a light heart and a connected spirit.

Superhero Endura: The embodiment of *adventure*, *persistence*, and *honesty*, Endura is the fearless explorer within, always ready to take on new challenges with unwavering determination. She inspires us to stay true to our path, even when the road is rough, and to live with honesty and integrity.

Superhero Halo: A figure of *love*, *compassion*, and *humanity*, Halo is the nurturing spirit who cares deeply for others, teaching us the power of empathy and the importance of self-care. She guides us to love unconditionally and to act with kindness in every interaction.

Superhero Harmony: The champion of *equality*, *cooperation*, and *leadership*, Harmony embodies the balance and fairness we seek in our relationships and communities. She urges us to lead with integrity, bringing people together and fostering environments where everyone can thrive. Harmony is the glue that binds us, reminding us of the power of unity and collaboration.

Superhero Sage: A muse of *insight*, *wisdom*, and *creativity*, Sage represents the deep thinker and the visionary in each of us. She encourages us to explore our inner wisdom, harness our creativity, and share our insights with the world. With

Sage in the driver's seat, we're guided by thoughtful reflection and a relentless pursuit of knowledge.

Superhero Serenity: The exemplar of *thoughtfulness*, *confidence*, and *humility*, Serenity brings a calm, peaceful confidence to every situation. She inspires us to act with grace, to be thoughtful in our decisions, and to remain humble in our achievements. Serenity is the quiet strength that helps us navigate life with poise and balance.

These snapshots provide a glimpse into the extraordinary potential within you, but there's so much more to discover. In the following sections, we will dive deeper into each superhero's defining elements: their superpowers (the core strengths they bring to the table), superwords (the empowering language that fuels their power), superstatements (affirmations that reinforce their strengths), superboosters (activities that amplify their energy), superdrainers (the obstacles and influences that weaken their power and drain their energy), and superpursuits (the pursuits that align with their essence and purpose).

What Are Superpowers?

We've already touched on the idea of superpowers, but let's take a closer look at what they really are. Superpowers are the unique strengths, abilities, and qualities that make you who you are. These are the innate talents or the skills you've developed over time that empower you to achieve your goals, overcome obstacles, and make a positive impact in the world around you. Each superpower you possess is a core capability — like resilience, empathy, leadership, or creativity — and these traits help you excel in your life's journey.

Superpowers aren't just about what you do well; they're about what makes you stand out. They are the extraordinary parts of your personality and character that shine brightly, even when life throws challenges your way. Your superpowers are the driving forces behind your actions, the qualities that others admire in you, and the strengths that help you navigate through both the mundane and the magnificent moments of life.

It's important to recognize that everyone's set of superpowers is different, and they evolve over time. Some may be more visible and celebrated, while others may be quieter but just as powerful. For example, you might be someone whose superpower is compassion, always finding ways to help others and make them feel valued. Or your superpower could be creativity, allowing you to see the world differently and come up with innovative solutions to problems.

Understanding and embracing your superpowers is not just about boosting your confidence — it's about harnessing these strengths to live a life that's true to you. When you fully recognize and tap into your superpowers, you unlock your potential and become a force for positive change in your own life and in the lives of those around you.

So, as we continue this journey of self-discovery, think about the superpowers that resonate with you. What are the qualities that have helped you overcome challenges, the skills that others turn to you for, and the traits that make you feel most alive? These are your superpowers, and they are waiting to be awakened and fully celebrated.

What Are Superwords?

Superwords are the powerful and vivid adjectives that define the very essence of your inner superhero. These words capture and express the core traits and characteristics that make your superhero unique. Think of superwords as the linguistic embodiment of your strengths or superpowers — each word is a concise, impactful descriptor that highlights the key attributes you possess.

Superwords are more than just descriptive terms; they are affirmations of who you are at your best. They succinctly convey the complexity of your abilities and personality, giving you a deeper understanding and appreciation of your unique qualities. These words resonate with the core of your being, reinforcing the strengths that you bring to the table in every aspect of your life.

For instance, if your superhero is Spark, your superwords include *optimistic*, *playful*, and *spiritual*. These words are not just random adjectives — they are a direct reflection of the light and joy that Spark brings to the world. They serve as reminders of your inherent capabilities and the positive energy you exude.

Superwords are also tools for empowerment. When you fully embrace these words, they become a part of your self-identity, helping you to align your thoughts, actions, and decisions with your true self. They are like a verbal shield, protecting you from self-doubt and empowering you to move forward with confidence and clarity.

These superwords will play a crucial role in chapter 4 when you create your personal Midlife Mantra. By combining these words into a powerful statement, you'll craft a mantra that encapsulates your essence and serves as a daily reminder of your strengths and purpose. This mantra will be your guiding light, ensuring that you stay connected to your superhero and continue to live in alignment with your true self.

What Are Superstatements?

Superstatements are empowering, affirming declarations that serve as a potent reminder of your identity and the strengths tied to your superpowers. These are concise, positive phrases crafted to foster a positive mindset, enhance your self-confidence, and reinforce your personal capabilities. Essentially, superstatements are like verbal affirmations that you can repeat to yourself regularly to stay motivated, resilient, and focused on your goals.

Think of superstatements as your personal mottoes — phrases you can turn to when you need an extra boost of confidence or a reminder of your inherent power. They act as a mental boost, helping you navigate through challenges by keeping you aligned with your true self and your unique abilities. Each superstatement is tailored to reflect the core qualities of its superhero, making it a personalized tool for empowerment.

For example, if your superhero is Endura, whose superpowers include adventure, persistence, and honesty, your superstatement is: "I am a fearless explorer, unwavering in my pursuit of truth and adventure. My strength lies in my honesty, persistence, and courage to face any challenge." This statement reinforces your ability to face challenges head-on with courage and integrity.

Here's how you can make the most of your superstatement:

- **Write it down:** Write your superstatement on a sticky note and put it somewhere you'll see it daily — like your bathroom mirror, your desk, or your car dashboard.
- **Say it daily:** Repeat your superstatement out loud every day, especially during times of doubt or stress. This regular affirmation will help you internalize the message, making it a core part of your self-identity.
- **Use it to manifest your potential:** Remember, thoughts become things. By consistently focusing on your superstatement, you'll start to radiate the energy it embodies, attracting more of what you desire into your life. It's a powerful tool for manifesting your goals and aligning your actions with your highest self.

As you move forward, let your superstatement be a phrase that centers you, inspires you, and propels you toward your most authentic and empowered life.

What Are Superboosters?

Now let's dive into the next superhero element: superboosters! They are the habits, practices, or actions that enhance and amplify your superpowers. Think of them as the fuel that powers your superhero engine, keeping your strengths at peak performance. By incorporating superboosters into your daily routine, you not only nurture and strengthen your superpowers but also increase their effectiveness in helping you navigate life's challenges and opportunities.

These superboosters are proactive steps you can take to maintain and elevate the positive traits that enable you to thrive. They're the little actions that, when practiced consistently, can lead to significant, transformative changes in your life.

For example, if one of your superpowers is compassion (associated with Superhero Halo), a superbooster might be practicing daily acts of kindness, volunteering, or engaging in mindfulness exercises that enhance your empathy and understanding of others. On the other hand, if creativity is your superpower (linked to Superhero Sage), a superbooster could be dedicating time each day to brainstorm new ideas, journal, or explore new artistic media.

Incorporating these superboosters into your life not only helps you maintain your superpowers but also leads you closer to discovering your true purpose and potential.

What Are Superdrainers?

Just as there are habits and practices that boost your strengths, there are also forces that drain them. These energy zappers, known as superdrainers, can slowly and sneakily weaken your abilities if left unchecked. Understanding what depletes your power is just as important as knowing how to enhance it — because even the strongest superheroes can be brought down by their kryptonite.

Superdrainers are the obstacles, habits, and external influences that sap your energy, dull your confidence, and hold you back from stepping fully into your power. They can take many forms — negative self-talk, toxic relationships, chronic stress, fear of failure, perfectionism, or even environments that stifle your growth. They often creep in unnoticed, making it harder to tap into your superpowers and pursue the life you truly want.

Superdrainers don't just slow you down; they can distort your sense of self, causing you to second-guess your abilities and shrink back from opportunities meant for you. Recognizing and managing these energy-draining forces is essential to maintaining your strengths. Just as a superhero wouldn't ignore the presence of kryptonite, you must be vigilant about identifying what drains you and actively take steps to minimize its influence.

We'll pinpoint the specific superdrainers that affect each superhero, empowering you to remove or neutralize them. Once you become aware of what's holding you back, you can take intentional action to redirect your energy toward what truly fuels you — your superpursuits.

What Are Superpursuits?

If you ever find yourself asking questions like "What is my purpose?" or "What is the best career for me?" understanding superpursuits will guide you toward the answers. Superpursuits are the activities — whether hobbies, careers, or essential life roles — that are perfectly aligned with your unique superpowers. These pursuits allow you to express and cultivate your core strengths in meaningful, fulfilling ways that contribute to your personal and professional growth, as well as your overall well-being.

While some superpursuits might look like traditional hobbies or careers — such as writing, painting, or leading a team — others are life-enriching roles that don't necessarily fit into those categories. For example, cooking delicious meals for yourself or your family is more than a hobby; it's an act of self-care and creativity. Parenting, caregiving, or mentoring might not be considered a career, but those pursuits are powerful expressions of compassion, leadership, and devotion that profoundly impact your life and the lives of others.

By engaging in superpursuits, you're not just doing what you enjoy; you're actively reinforcing the traits that make you who you are, nurturing your well-being, and moving closer to your full potential. These activities resonate with your core qualities, ensuring that the time and energy you invest in them directly contribute to your journey of self-discovery, mastery, and fulfillment.

Whether you're channeling your creativity into crafting, nurturing your compassion through caregiving, or strengthening your sense of purpose by volunteering, superpursuits help you live in harmony with your strengths and values. They're not one-size-fits-all. Just as each superhero has distinct superpowers, the activities that bring you joy and fulfillment will be unique to you.

Take it from someone who spent years pursuing hobbies and careers that were misaligned with her strengths and true calling — I was miserable. But once I embraced my superhero within, Superhero Spark, I began to engage in activities that truly fed my soul. Now every day feels like I'm living in alignment with my purpose, and I want the same for you.

Your superpursuits are a crucial aspect of living a balanced and harmonious life. They are the gateway to a life that is not only fulfilling but also deeply resonant with who you truly are. With the guidance of the Superhero Guide, I hope you will be inspired to explore and embrace the pursuits that light you up, whether they're hobbies, life roles, or anything in between.

 Take the Superhero Quiz

Are you ready to discover which of the Spectacular Six Superheroes you embody? Accessible at MySuperheroQuiz.com, this engaging quiz is designed to reveal the superhero that reflects your unique strengths and personality.

Once you've discovered your superhero, flip to her section of the Superhero Guide below to explore the corresponding elements that will guide you on your journey to fully awaken your inner superhero. Remember, embracing your strengths isn't just about personal fulfillment — it's about cultivating resilience and navigating the challenges of midlife with grace and power. So grab your cape and get ready to soar to new heights!

My superhero is ________________________.

The Superhero Guide

Superhero Spark: Optimism, Playfulness, Spirituality

Spark superpowers: Superhero Spark exudes an aura of positivity that instantly brightens the mood of anyone in her presence. She has a deep connection to her higher self and the sacred. As a highly sensitive individual, she can tune in to the emotions of others, providing comfort and understanding. Superhero Spark's unwavering optimism gives her the strength to overcome obstacles and maintain hope in the face of adversity. With her mindfulness superpower, Superhero Spark stays grounded in the present moment, making the most of every situation. Spark's appreciation for art and talent allows her to inspire creativity in others. Superhero Spark excels at transforming negative energy into positive vibrations.

Spark superwords: animated, blissful, breezy, bright, buoyant, charismatic, charming, cheerful, dynamic, elated, energetic, engaging, enthusiastic, exuberant, fun-loving, gleeful, grateful, heartwarming, hopeful, imaginative, inspiring, jovial, joyful, jubilant, lighthearted, lively, merry, optimistic, playful, positive, radiant, refreshing, soulful, sparkling, spirited, spiritual, uplifting, vibrant, vivacious, whimsical, zesty

Spark superstatements: "I am a radiant beacon of optimism, playfulness, and spirituality. My light shines brightly, transforming the world with joy, hope, and love."

Spark superboosters: Starting her day with a mindfulness meditation practice can help Superhero Spark strengthen her spiritual connection and maintain a calm, focused mindset throughout the day. Spending time in nature can rejuvenate Superhero Spark's energy and inspire her appreciation for the world's wonders, enhancing her ability to spread positivity. Pursuing creative hobbies like painting, writing, or music can fuel her creative inspiration and keep her spirit vibrant and expressive. Regularly engaging in energy-cleansing practices, such as using sage, sound baths, or crystals, can help her maintain a clear and positive aura.

Spark superdrainers: Negativity can quickly dim Spark's light, making it harder for her to maintain optimism and uplift others. Overwhelm from taking on too much without boundaries can drain her playful energy and leave her emotionally exhausted. Disconnection from her spiritual side, such as by neglecting mindfulness, can make her feel ungrounded, while stagnation — falling into routines without creative or new experiences — can dull her enthusiasm. Self-doubt can cast a shadow over her hopeful resilience, and prolonged exposure to cynicism can shake her faith in humanity's potential for goodness.

Spark superpursuits:

- *Hobbies:* performing arts (theater, dance), creative writing or poetry, playing musical instruments, stand-up comedy, meditation and yoga, traveling to vibrant and exotic locations, social dancing (salsa, swing), stand-up paddleboarding, digital art or graphic design, meditation, spiritual or creativity retreats, joining fun runs — themed events focused on movement and community
- *Careers:* event planner, motivational speaker, life coach, children's book author, music therapist, spiritual leader or adviser, animator, graphic designer, youth counselor, retreat coordinator, professional entertainer or comedian

- *Life roles:*
  - *Parent or caregiver:* Bringing joy and optimism to parenting or caregiving by fostering a playful, nurturing environment.
  - *Friendship connector:* Acting as the glue in social circles, uplifting friends with lighthearted and vibrant energy.
  - *Community builder:* Organizing local gatherings, clubs, or events that inspire creativity, connection, and positivity.
  - *Mentor or guide:* Offering spiritual or emotional support to others, helping them discover their inner light and navigate challenges with optimism.
  - *Celebration planner:* Infusing everyday moments with celebration and fun — whether hosting family dinners, holiday parties, or creative date nights.

Superhero Endura: Adventure, Persistence, Honesty

Endura superpowers: Superhero Endura has the bravery to act on her convictions, face challenges head-on, and stand up for what is right, even in the face of opposition or danger. Endura's persistence shines through her ability to finish what she starts, overcome obstacles, and remain steadfast in her goals, despite any setbacks or discouragements. She values truth, keeps her promises, and maintains integrity, ensuring that she is consistent and true to herself in all aspects of life. Endura approaches life with enthusiasm and vitality, treating each day as an adventure. Endura's love for adventure drives her to explore the unknown and embark on truth-seeking journeys. She encourages others to be true to themselves and pursue their goals with courage.

Endura superwords: adventurous, assertive, bold, brave, committed, conscientious, courageous, dependable, determined, direct, dynamic, enduring, fearless, firm, focused, forthright, gritty, grounded, hardy, honest, indomitable, persistent, principled, reliable, resilient, robust, rugged, solid, steadfast, strong, sturdy, tenacious, tireless, true, trustworthy, unstoppable, unswerving, unyielding, valiant, vigorous

Endura superstatements: "I am a fearless explorer, unwavering in my pursuit of truth and adventure. My strength lies in my honesty, persistence, and courage to face any challenge."

Endura superboosters: Regular physical activity can enhance Endura's vitality and endurance, preparing her for any physical challenges that come her way. Setting clear, achievable goals can help Endura maintain her focus and persistence, ensuring she stays on track with her objectives. Regularly planning new adventures or challenges can keep Endura's sense of exploration and excitement alive, fueling her adventurous spirit. Practicing resilience-building techniques, such as stress management and positive thinking, can enhance Endura's ability to bounce back from setbacks.

Endura superdrainers: Procrastination can stall Endura's momentum, making it harder for her to follow through on her goals and maintain her persistence. A lack of physical activity or adventure can sap her energy, leaving her feeling stagnant and uninspired. Overwhelm from taking on too much without setting boundaries can wear down her endurance, leading to frustration and exhaustion. Fear of failure can make her hesitant to take the bold risks necessary for growth, while rigid thinking can prevent her from adapting to life's unexpected challenges. Finally, pessimism — whether from others or within herself — can cloud her adventurous spirit and diminish her drive to push forward.

Endura superpursuits:

- *Hobbies:* rock climbing or mountaineering, marathon running or triathlons, adventure travel, woodworking or metalworking, survival skills training, historical reenactment, extreme sports (BASE jumping, paragliding, etc.), long-distance cycling, off-road motorcycling, building or restoring cars, tactical games like paintball

- *Careers:* adventure tour guide, military or law enforcement officer, sports coach or personal trainer, crisis management expert, archaeologist, entrepreneur in challenging industries, expedition leader, professional athlete, firefighter, wilderness survival instructor, automotive engineer
- *Life roles:*
    - *Protector or advocate:* Acting as a champion for others, standing up for what's right, and advocating for justice in her community or family.
    - *Mentor or guide:* Supporting others on their journeys and encouraging persistence and resilience by sharing her honest insights and experiences.
    - *Trailblazer:* Leading the way in new ventures, whether exploring a literal trail in the wilderness or forging a new path in her family, community, or workplace.
    - *Family adventurer:* Inspiring loved ones to embrace adventure; planning trips, outdoor activities, or challenges that strengthen bonds and create lasting memories.
    - *Caretaker of truth:* Upholding honesty and integrity in her relationships and responsibilities, ensuring others feel safe, valued, and understood.

Superhero Halo: Love, Compassion, Humanity

Halo superpowers: Superhero Halo deeply understands and can share the feelings of others, offering comfort and support to those in need. She goes out of her way to help, support, and care for others, often putting their needs above her own. Halo's heart is filled with unconditional love that she freely shares with those around her. She is driven by a desire to make the world a better place for all. Halo is tuned in to her surroundings and can sense what people need, even before they ask. While Halo is loving and caring, she also knows how to protect her heart. Halo is aware of her own feelings and those of others, allowing her to navigate complex emotional landscapes with grace and understanding.

Halo superwords: affectionate, altruistic, amiable, benevolent, caring, charitable, compassionate, considerate, devoted, empathetic, forgiving, friendly, generous, gentle, good-natured, gracious, healing, heartening, helpful, humane, inspirational, kindhearted, loving, merciful, nurturing, patient, peaceful, philanthropic, selfless, sincere, softhearted, supportive, sweet, sympathetic, tender, thoughtful, understanding, warm, welcoming

Halo superstatements: "I am a beacon of love, compassion, and humanity. My heart overflows with kindness, and I radiate empathy and warmth, touching the lives of all beings with gentle grace."

Halo superboosters: Participating in volunteer activities that align with her values can reinforce Halo's humanitarian spirit and commitment to making a difference. Prioritizing self-care practices that nurture her emotional well-being can ensure that Halo maintains her capacity to care for others. Exploring and learning about different cultures and perspectives can broaden Halo's understanding of humanity and deepen her empathy. Establishing healthy boundaries can protect Halo's energy and ensure that she can continue to offer love and compassion without depleting herself.

Halo superdrainers: Neglecting self-care can leave Halo emotionally drained, reducing her ability to offer love and compassion to others. Overextending herself by taking on too many responsibilities can lead to burnout, making it difficult to maintain her nurturing spirit. Toxic relationships or constantly giving without receiving support in return can deplete her emotional reserves and make her feel unappreciated. Suppressing her own emotions or failing to set healthy boundaries can leave her feeling overwhelmed and disconnected from her true self. Being surrounded by cynicism or negativity can weaken her faith in humanity, while isolation can diminish her sense of purpose and ability to uplift others.

Halo superpursuits:

- *Hobbies:* volunteering for charitable organizations, gardening, animal care, cooking and baking for friends and family, crafting, knitting or sewing, practicing mindfulness and compassion meditation, participating in community service projects, participating in community choirs, handcrafting gifts, leading support groups, peer mentoring
- *Careers:* social worker or counselor, nurse or healthcare provider, nonprofit organization leader, teacher or educator, veterinarian or pet rescue organizer, human rights advocate, pediatrician, marriage and family therapist, charity fundraiser, hospice worker, community outreach coordinator
- *Life roles:*
    - *Caregiver:* Providing emotional and physical support to loved ones, children, or elders and fostering a nurturing and loving environment.
    - *Community builder:* Creating connections in her neighborhood or social circles by organizing acts of kindness, community events, or support networks.
    - *Peacemaker:* Acting as a mediator in conflicts, offering empathy and understanding to bridge divides and bring people together.
    - *Mentor or counselor:* Guiding others through challenges with patience, wisdom, and a listening ear, helping them grow and heal.
    - *Humanitarian advocate:* Speaking up for those in need,

advocating for social justice, and contributing to causes that make the world a better place.

Superhero Harmony: Equality, Cooperation, Leadership

Harmony superpowers: Superhero Harmony can lead with a deep sense of self-awareness and empathy, ensuring that all voices are heard and valued. Harmony champions equality, treating everyone with fairness and impartiality. She excels in teamwork, contributing actively to the success of her team or group. Harmony is committed to being a responsible citizen, actively participating in her community and partnering with others to effect positive change. Her leadership style is empowering, inspiring others to take initiative and contribute their best. Harmony has a knack for resolving conflicts in a way that promotes understanding and reconciliation. Harmony leads with a clear vision for a more inclusive and cooperative world.

Harmony superwords: accommodating, balanced, collaborative, conscientious, cooperative, cordial, democratic, diplomatic, empowering, equitable, ethical, facilitative, fair, guiding, harmonious, impartial, inclusive, influential, inspiring, integrative, just, mediating, motivational, organized, peacemaking, persuasive, principled, reconciling, respectful, strategic, supportive, tactful, team-oriented, transparent, trust-building, unifying, visionary, wise

Harmony superstatements: "I am a beacon of equality, cooperation, and leadership. I lead with inclusivity, inspire collaboration, and champion fairness, fostering a world where everyone is valued and united in purpose."

Harmony superboosters: Participating in team-building activities can strengthen Harmony's ability to work well with others and promote a cooperative spirit. Learning about different cultures, backgrounds, and viewpoints can broaden Harmony's understanding of equality and enhance her inclusive leadership. Volunteering in her community can reinforce Harmony's commitment to teamwork and civic engagement. Building relationships with other leaders and changemakers can provide Harmony with inspiration and support for her own leadership journey.

Harmony superdrainers: Operating in environments that lack collaboration or undervalue teamwork can weaken Harmony's ability to foster cooperation and create positive change. Unresolved conflicts or exclusionary practices can disrupt her sense of fairness and inclusivity, making it difficult for her to unite others. Rigid thinking and ignoring diverse perspectives can hinder her ability to adapt and lead effectively. Neglecting self-care can lead to burnout, reducing her capacity to lead with strength and fairness, while micromanagement can stifle her creativity and collaborative spirit. Finally, witnessing pessimism or injustice without taking action can diminish her belief in equality and weaken her motivation to advocate for change.

Harmony superpursuits:

- *Hobbies:* team sports such as soccer or basketball, debate club or public speaking, community theater, playing in a band or orchestra, choral directing or group music activities, volunteer work involving team coordination, cultural exchange programs, organizing community sports leagues, participating in Model United Nations, serving on local committees, hosting exchange students
- *Careers:* diplomat or mediator, corporate trainer or human resources manager, project manager, politician or community organizer, social enterprise founder, diversity and inclusion officer, labor union leader, conflict resolution specialist, community planner, public administration professional

- *Life roles:*
  - *Community organizer:* Bringing people together to tackle challenges, promote inclusivity, and create positive change within her neighborhood or society.
  - *Team facilitator:* Acting as a unifying presence in groups, ensuring everyone's voice is heard and fostering an environment of mutual respect and collaboration.
  - *Family mediator:* Resolving conflicts with fairness and empathy, helping family members navigate disagreements while strengthening their bonds.
  - *Mentor or coach:* Guiding others to discover their own leadership potential and encouraging teamwork and cooperation in personal or professional growth.
  - *Champion of inclusion:* Advocating for fairness and equality in all areas of life, from supporting marginalized voices to creating opportunities for diverse participation.

Superhero Sage: Insight, Wisdom, Creativity

Sage superpowers: Superhero Sage has the ability to think outside the box, generating original ideas and innovative solutions. Sage is open to new experiences and ideas, which fuels her creativity and curiosity. She is not afraid to take risks and venture into the unknown, which leads to personal growth and discovery. Sage weighs all aspects objectively when making decisions. Her love of learning is not just about curiosity but also about mastering new skills and expanding her expertise. Sage has the ability to see the bigger picture and offer insightful advice. Sage is a source of inspiration, encouraging others to think creatively and pursue their own paths of discovery. Sage's creativity and curiosity make her adaptable to new situations.

Sage superwords: analytical, artistic, astute, clever, creative, cultured, curious, deep, enlightened, experienced, genius, groundbreaking, imaginative, ingenious, innovative, insightful, intellectual, intuitive, inventive, knowledgeable, learned, masterful, original, perceptive, philosophical, profound, prudent, reflective, resourceful, savvy, scholarly, shrewd, skillful, sophisticated, thoughtful, versatile, visionary, wise

Sage superstatements: "I am a wellspring of insight, wisdom, and creativity. My mind is open to endless possibilities, and I embrace each day as an opportunity to learn, grow, and inspire."

Sage superboosters: Engaging in regular creative activities, such as writing, painting, or playing music, can keep Sage's creative spark alive and encourage the flow of new ideas. Actively seeking out different viewpoints and engaging in conversations with people from various backgrounds can broaden Sage's understanding and enhance her ability to offer insightful advice. Keeping a journal to record ideas and insights can help Sage organize her thoughts and track her personal growth. Connecting with other creative individuals can provide Sage with inspiration, collaboration opportunities, and a sense of community.

Sage superdrainers: A creative block or lack of inspiration can leave Sage feeling stuck, hindering her ability to generate new ideas and solutions. Neglecting self-care is one factor that can cloud her mental clarity and creativity. Intellectual stagnation — an absence of new knowledge or challenges — can dull her curiosity and love of learning. Overthinking can lead to paralysis by analysis, preventing her from taking action, while information overload can overwhelm her, making it difficult for her to discern what truly matters. Closed-mindedness can limit her ability to grow and offer fresh insights. Finally, fear of failure can make her hesitant to take risks.

Sage superpursuits:

- *Hobbies:* painting, drawing, sculpting, writing books or articles, chess or strategic games, photography, philosophy or book clubs, attending lectures or cultural events, stargazing or amateur astronomy, collecting and restoring antiques, homebrewing or winemaking, hosting a podcast on thought-provoking topics, experimental cooking or molecular gastronomy

- *Careers:* academic researcher or professor, creative director or designer, writer or journalist, inventor, scientist, consultant in various fields, art curator or critic, museum curator, futurist, patent lawyer, cultural anthropologist, professional consultant in creative industries
- *Life roles:*
    - *Mentor or adviser:* Sharing wisdom and guidance with others, helping them navigate challenges and discover their own potential.
    - *Creative visionary:* Designing innovative solutions or projects in her family, community, or workplace, inspiring others with her originality.
    - *Life learner:* Continuously seeking out new knowledge, experiences, and skills to enrich her understanding and grow as a person.
    - *Family historian:* Curating and preserving meaningful stories, traditions, or artifacts that connect loved ones to their roots and inspire future generations.
    - *Cultural connector:* Bringing people together through shared appreciation for art, philosophy, or cultural experiences, fostering deeper connections and insights.

Superhero Serenity: Thoughtfulness, Confidence, Humility

Serenity superpowers: Superhero Serenity controls her appetites and emotions, maintaining a sense of balance and discipline in her life. Serenity possesses a quiet confidence in her ability to achieve her goals. She acts with caution and foresight, considering the long-term consequences of her actions and decisions. Serenity is aware of her strengths and talents but remains humble, not seeking the spotlight or excessive recognition. Serenity is forgiving and accepting of others' mistakes. Her thoughtfulness extends to her interactions with others, as she considers their feelings and perspectives. Serenity's confidence and humility are underpinned by an inner strength that allows her to face adversity with calmness and resilience.

Serenity superwords: assured, calm, composed, confident, considerate, contemplative, controlled, deliberate, diligent, discerning, discreet, gentle, gracious, grounded, humble, introspective, levelheaded, measured, modest, patient, poised, prudent, refined, reflective, reserved, respectful, secure, self-assured, serene, sincere, stoic, subtle, tactful, thoughtful, tranquil, unassuming, understanding, unpretentious

Serenity superstatements: "I am a beacon of thoughtfulness, confidence, and humility. I navigate life with inner strength, consider the well-being of others, and embrace each moment with a serene and modest heart."

Serenity superboosters: Writing in a journal can provide Serenity with an opportunity to reflect on her goals, achievements, and challenges, fostering her self-awareness and humility. Setting and achieving small goals can boost Serenity's confidence in her abilities and reinforce her belief in her effectiveness. Volunteering or engaging in acts of service can keep Serenity grounded in humility and focused on the well-being of others. Taking time for personal reflection can help Serenity maintain a sense of modesty and gratitude for her accomplishments.

Serenity superdrainers: Emotional reactivity and impulsiveness can disrupt Serenity's ability to remain calm and thoughtful, weakening her self-regulation. Overconfidence or allowing pride to overshadow humility can create an imbalance, diminishing her self-awareness.

Holding grudges can erode her forgiving nature, while isolation may disconnect her from the meaningful relationships that nurture her thoughtfulness. Neglecting self-care can lead to burnout, making it difficult to maintain her composed and resilient demeanor. Finally, relying too much on external validation or avoiding self-reflection can hinder her personal growth and ability to navigate life with quiet confidence and grace.

Serenity superpursuits:

- *Hobbies:* yoga or tai chi, hiking, bird-watching, reading and studying various subjects, journaling or blogging, tea crafting and tasting, pottery or other calming crafts, ikebana (Japanese flower arranging), calligraphy, meditation teaching, pilgrimage trekking, classic literature book clubs
- *Careers:* psychologist or therapist, meditation instructor or wellness coach, librarian or archivist, environmental scientist, philosopher or theologian, fine artist or photographer, diplomatic service officer, Zen garden designer, executive coach focusing on mindful leadership, conservator or restorer of historic sites, ethical banking specialist
- *Life roles:*
    - *Peacekeeper:* Acting as a calming presence in family, social, or professional settings, helping to de-escalate tensions and foster understanding.
    - *Reflective guide:* Supporting others by offering thoughtful advice and quiet encouragement, helping them navigate life's challenges with grace.
    - *Steward of the environment:* Caring for nature through mindful practices, such as gardening, conservation efforts, or eco-friendly initiatives.
    - *Caring listener:* Being a compassionate and attentive ear for friends or loved ones, offering support without judgment or need of recognition.

- *Personal anchor:* Creating balance and stability for her family or community by modeling resilience, humility, and calm leadership during challenging times.

Coming Up

As you wrap up this chapter, remember that your superhero is not just a figure of imagination; she is a vital part of who you are. By rediscovering and empowering your unique superpowers, you are not only reigniting your passion and purpose but also equipping yourself with the resilience to navigate midlife with confidence and grace. Embrace the journey ahead, knowing that your superhero is ready to take on whatever challenges come your way. The next chapter of your life is in your hands, and it's going to be nothing short of extraordinary.

As you continue your journey of midlife transformation, it's time to turn inward and strengthen the most important relationship you'll ever have — the one with yourself. In the next chapter, you'll learn how to become your own best friend by mastering the art of self-talk. Your mind can be your greatest ally or your harshest critic, and the choice is yours. With my Stop, Drop, and Roll method, you'll gain practical tools to silence the negativity and cultivate a mindset that supports your growth, happiness, and inner peace. Get ready to transform your thinking and, in turn, transform your life.

3

BECOME YOUR OWN BFF

Change your thoughts and you change your world.
— Norman Vincent Peale, *The Power of Positive Thinking*

Starting over in a new city with a new job seemed so refreshing to me because it let me leave behind an old life filled with panic attacks, poor health, and crappy relationships. Or so I thought. I soon realized that no matter where I went, my problems came with me. If anything, the lonely nights I spent in bed in Chicago staring at the ceiling fan intensified my troubles and trauma. Thousands of thoughts swirled around in my mind to the point that I would become nauseous, break out in a cold sweat, and end up with a massive migraine. If I was lucky enough to fall asleep, I would immediately go into a horrible nightmare of watching my brother take his last breath.

As I lay on a pillow soaked with tears, my alarm would annoyingly go off, and I would begin my day already feeling exhausted — not a great way to start a new job. With no sleep, aching joints, and a throbbing head, I would stumble to the bathroom to wash my face. The tired and miserable woman in the mirror staring back at me was not the badass superhero I had envisioned. Instead, she was my vicious enemy.

Shaking her head in disappointment, she said to me, *Look at you, you're a disgrace. You look like shit, you feel like shit, and you are shit. I can't believe you left everything behind to try to create some fairy-tale life. What were you thinking?*

Like an autoimmune disease attacking the body, the woman in the mirror was attacking me. And then it hit me — *I* was attacking me. I had become my worst enemy. It wasn't so much that my problems had followed me, but more that *I* was the problem. I was the culprit behind the chaos.

I realized the solution to my problem was staring me in the face. Literally. If I was the problem, then I could be the solution. If I had become my worst enemy, then I could become my best friend. If I had the power to create negativity, then I had the power to create positivity. That was it right there: I had the power to control the swirling thoughts in my mind that were controlling my life.

Looking back at the woman in the mirror with fresh, new eyes, I began singing my version of Michael Jackson's song "Man in the Mirror":

I'm starting with the woman in the mirror
I'm asking her to change her ways
And no message could've been any clearer
If you wanna make your world a better place
Take a look at yourself and then make a change

Though all the steps I had taken thus far to change my life were improvements, changing my mind would make the greatest impact of them all. It was time to stop hating myself and being my worst critic and time to start loving myself and being my greatest cheerleader. It's your time too.

The Battle in Your Mind

Your mind is either your best friend or your worst enemy, and either way, it's the one leading you through your life. You create your thoughts, and your thoughts create your life. In other words, your internal world dictates your external world. Only one person controls your mind, and that is you. You control your destiny.

Think of your mind like a garden. Each thought you have is a seed you plant. Negative thoughts — like self-doubt, envy, or regret — are weeds that grow wild and choke the life out of the flowers. Positive thoughts — like kindness, joy, and hope — are the beautiful blooms that make the garden a place of peace and fulfillment.

Now, here's the catch: Whatever you water is what grows. Are you watering the weeds with constant criticism, comparison, and self-doubt? Or are you nurturing the flowers with encouraging words, self-compassion, and gratitude?

The choice is yours. You have the power to tend your mental garden with care, pulling out the weeds when they appear and giving extra sunlight to the flowers that reflect your best self. The more you nurture positivity, the more your inner world will blossom, and you'll start to see those blooms reflected in your outer world too.

If you want to create a life you love, you need to starve the weeds of negativity and instead nourish the flowers of positivity. By being a conscious gardener and carefully tending to the thoughts running through your mind, you can transform your inner critic into a loving inner coach. Of course, that's easier said than done. That's why I'll share my Stop, Drop, and Roll method — three simple steps to stop negative thoughts in their tracks and help you change your stinkin' thinkin'. Just like the fire safety technique you learned as a kid, the Stop, Drop, and Roll method will help you escape the fire of negativity. Let's go, firewoman!

Stop, Drop, and Roll

The Stop, Drop, and Roll method is designed to help you become your own best friend by changing negative self-talk into positive affirmations.

Step 1: Stop

Close your eyes and take a deep breath in. Slowly exhale. As you begin to settle your body, watch the ticker tape of thoughts running across your mind. Don't judge your thoughts; just observe them. The moment you notice a negative thought entering your mind, imagine a stop sign in front of you. This is your signal to pause. Take a deep breath in through your nose and slowly exhale through your mouth. Acknowledge the negative thought that has entered your mind. This step is crucial as it brings awareness to the thought instead of letting it run on autopilot. Say to yourself, "I recognize this thought." For example, if the thought is *I'm not good enough*, recognize it by saying, "I see you, *I'm not good enough*."

Step 2: Drop

Imagine the negative thought as a hot coal in your hand. Feel the heat and the discomfort it brings. Visualize dropping the negative thought. Watch it fall away and disappear. Take a deep breath in and exhale, releasing any remaining physical tension associated with the negative thought and consciously relax those areas of your body. For example, as you drop the thought *I'm not good enough*, see it vanish and feel a sense of relief.

Step 3: Roll

Now roll in a new, positive and empowering thought. Think of a positive affirmation or a kind, encouraging thought that counters the negative one. Visualize this new thought as a beautiful, glowing light. For example, replace *I'm not good enough* with *I am capable and worthy*. Visualize *I am capable and worthy* as a warm, glowing light entering your mind and spreading throughout your body, filling you with warmth and positivity. Repeat the positive affirmation to yourself several times.

Take a final deep breath in and slowly exhale. Take a moment to reflect on how you feel after transforming the negative thought into a positive one. When you're ready, gently open your eyes and bring your awareness back to the present moment.

Practice Regularly

Make it a habit to practice the Stop, Drop, and Roll method whenever negative thoughts arise, and watch how your mindset transforms. As you tune in to your self-talk, you'll start to notice how loud and intrusive those negative thoughts can be — almost like unruly party crashers in your mind. They're your cue to grab your stop sign!

By stopping to recognize the negativity, dropping it like it's hot, and rolling in fresh, positive thoughts, you can build a kinder, more supportive relationship with yourself. It's not about perfection; it's about progress. Each time you consciously redirect your thoughts, you strengthen the habit of positivity and self-compassion.

The key is to bring awareness to your thoughts as often as you can throughout the day. Of course, with thousands upon thousands of thoughts racing through your mind daily, it's nearly impossible to monitor every single one. That's okay. The goal isn't to control every thought, but to gently steer your mindset in a more positive direction over time.

To truly transform your mindset and harness the power of positive thinking, you need to connect with a deeper energy — a calm, steady force that goes beyond the endless chatter of your mind. This is where meditation comes in. Meditation allows you to quiet your thoughts and tap into an inner reservoir of strength, clarity, and peace. It's like pressing the Reset button for your mind and soul.

Ready to access this incredible energy? Let's dive into how meditation can help you elevate your life.

Tap into Your Energy

Energy is everything, and everything is energy. In fact, atoms, including those in the human body, are made up of 99.99999 percent energy and only 0.00001 percent matter. Why is this significant? Because tapping into this invisible energy can make your dreams visible. It has the power to transform your life from ordinary to extraordinary. So how do you connect with this miraculous energy? The answer is simple: meditation. By connecting with your soul through meditation, you can unlock a profound source of strength and clarity.

The Benefits of Meditation

Meditation offers numerous benefits that can transform your life, especially in midlife, when stress levels often rise, hormones fluctuate, and the demands of caregiving, career shifts, aging parents, and self-reflection all seem to collide at once. Here are some key advantages:

- **Reduced stress and anxiety:** Meditation helps calm the mind and minimize the stress hormones in your body, promoting a sense of peace and relaxation.
- **Greater focus and concentration:** Regular practice can enhance your attention span and cognitive abilities, making it easier to stay focused on your goals.
- **Improved emotional health:** By instilling a deeper connection with yourself, meditation can improve your emotional well-being and help you process difficult emotions.
- **Enhanced self-awareness:** Meditation fosters self-reflection, helping you understand your thoughts and behavior better, leading to personal growth.
- **More robust physical health:** It can lower blood pressure, improve sleep, and boost your immune system.

Starting Your Meditation Practice

By incorporating meditation into your daily routine, you can harness the power of your energy, transform your mindset, and step into the extraordinary life you are meant to live. Beginning a meditation practice can seem daunting, but it's simpler than you might think. Here are some steps to get started:

1. **Find a quiet space:** Choose a peaceful environment where you won't be disturbed.
2. **Set a timer:** Start with just five to ten minutes a day and gradually increase the duration as you become more comfortable.
3. **Focus on your breath:** Pay attention to your breathing. Notice the sensation of the air entering and leaving your body.
4. **Let go of judgments:** Don't worry if your mind wanders. Gently bring your focus back to your breath without judgment.
5. **Practice regularly:** Consistency is key. Aim to meditate at the same time each day to build a habit.

Creating New Neural Pathways

Meditation can help you create new neural pathways by replacing old, limiting beliefs with new, empowering ones. This ability is known as neuroplasticity, and it allows your brain to rewire itself based on your experiences and thoughts. Through meditation, you can:

- **identify limiting beliefs:** Become aware of the negative thoughts that hold you back.
- **introduce empowering beliefs:** Use positive affirmations and visualization during meditation to instill supportive new beliefs.

- **reinforce new pathways:** Consistently practicing meditation strengthens these new neural pathways, making empowering beliefs your new default.

Complimentary Midlife Meditation Audio Series

To support you on this journey, I offer a complimentary FREEDOM Meditation Series. Accessible at WomenWakingUp.com, this audio collection includes seven guided meditations corresponding to the seven steps to FREEDOM. These meditations are designed to help you tap into your energy, align with your true self, and empower you to thrive in midlife. Now that you have completed step 1, you can listen to the Free Yourself meditation to help you become your own best friend by learning to manage your thoughts and transform negative self-talk into positive, empowering affirmations.

Coming Up

We will keep the momentum of energy flowing into chapter 4, "Step into the New You," where I'll guide you through the Design the New You exercise. This powerful visualization practice will help you connect deeply with the woman you are becoming. Think of it as a rehearsal for your future self, where every thought, feeling, and behavior aligns with the version of you that is already thriving. By stepping into the new you today, you'll begin living in alignment with the life you are destined to create.

But that's not all. To wrap up chapter 4, you'll craft your very own Midlife Mantra — a powerful sentence packed with your action steps, intentions, superpowers, and goals. This mantra will serve as your guiding light, keeping you focused and inspired as you continue on your journey.

STEP

RESET YOUR LIFE

4

STEP INTO THE NEW YOU

You have to believe in yourself when no one else does — that makes you a winner right there.

— attributed to Venus Williams

Depressed, insecure, and frightened — these words perfectly encapsulated the forty-five-year-old Wendy who dreamed of driving an RV into the desert sunset. At the time, I was broke, divorced, and unhealthy, and achieving this BHAG (Big Hairy Audacious Goal, a term coined by Jim Collins and Jerry I. Porras in their book *Built to Last*) seemed like a distant fantasy. It felt impossible to reach as long as I remained trapped in the cycle of fear and misery that had defined my life for so long.

The reality was that in order to buy my house on wheels, I'd have to sell a lot of houses at my new job in Chicago. This endeavor demanded an enormous amount of my time, energy, and focus. In addition to the financial means, this goal necessitated a healthy body to endure the long work hours, emotional stability to navigate living alone in an unfamiliar city, and a positive mindset to carry me through these wild adventures. To succeed, I needed to transform from a woman who was depressed, insecure, and frightened into one who was strong, confident, and courageous. And I needed to make that transformation immediately.

I had moved a thousand miles away from friends and family to start fresh in a new city and a new job, so there was no time to wallow in fragility or fear. It was go time! But how could I shift so dramatically from a state of misery to a state of joy? The answer lay in three powerful words: *Act as if.*

I had to act as if my future self — the brave, bold, and badass woman I aspired to be — was already here, fully present and in command. I had to step into the shoes of my superhero every single day until I *became* that superhero. Like an actress preparing for a role, I needed to immerse myself in the thoughts, feelings, and actions of this future self. How did she sleep at night? What did she eat? How did she enter a room? What did she do for fun and relaxation? How did she dress? What did she say to herself when she looked in the mirror?

Who had the answers to all these questions? I did. The realization was exhilarating — I had the power to design and become the woman I wanted to be. The power to create this extraordinary woman was within me all along. And guess what? The same power is within you too.

 Design the New You

To create a new life, you need to think, feel, and act like the person you are becoming. It's time to put pen to paper and bring the new you to life — the version of you who is already living her dreams with confidence and clarity. In this journaling exercise, you will step into your future self and envision how she navigates her life with purpose and joy. Set aside any doubts, fears, or limiting beliefs, because there are no boundaries to who you can become. Answer the questions below, writing as the woman you truly want to be, embracing her strengths, mindset, and energy. You are both the creator and the creation. Let's begin!

Morning Rituals

- As the new you, how do you start your day? What habits or rituals set a positive tone for your morning?
- What mindset and energy do you want to embody each morning to feel empowered and ready to take on the day?

Body Image and Self-Perception

- As the new you, how do you feel in your body? Describe the confidence and emotions you experience daily.
- What healthy habits does the new you practice to stay strong, vibrant, and energized?

Self-Care and Wellness

- How does the new you prioritize self-care? What daily practices keep you physically, mentally, and emotionally balanced?
- Which wellness rituals help you feel grounded and connected to yourself throughout the day?

Professional Fulfillment

- What kind of work excites and fulfills the new you? How does it align with your values and passions?
- How do you show up in your career as your best self, feeling confident, capable, and valued?

Relationships and Connections

- Who are the people that surround the new you? How do these relationships support and uplift you?
- How do you bring your best self into your relationships, fostering meaningful and loving connections?

Personal Growth and Learning

- How does the new you continue to grow and evolve? What new skills or knowledge are you committed to mastering?
- In what ways do you challenge yourself to step out of your comfort zone and embrace growth?

Creativity and Passion Projects

- How does the new you express creativity? What passion projects ignite your joy and fulfillment?
- How do you nurture your creative self, balancing passion projects with the rest of your life?

Evening Wind-Down

- As the new you, how do you end your day? What rituals help you unwind, reflect, and restore your energy?
- How do you ensure restful sleep, waking up rejuvenated and ready to embrace the day ahead?

Future Vision

- Fast-forward five years. How has the new you evolved? What accomplishments and experiences have shaped you into this future self?
- What legacy do you want to create, and how does living as the new you help you make that vision a reality?

Barriers and Solutions

- What current habits or beliefs are holding you back? How can you overcome these barriers to fully embody the new you?
- What actionable steps can you take today to align more closely with the new you?

Reflection and Gratitude

- At the end of each day, what is the new you most grateful for? How does gratitude influence your mindset and overall well-being?
- How do you celebrate your progress and honor the transformation into the new you?

The New You Meditation

If you're feeling a bit of writer's cramp, take it as a good sign — it means you're making yourself a priority, and the new you is already starting to take shape. Reflecting deeply on your desires, goals, and daily habits will help you create a clear and actionable vision of the woman you aspire to become in midlife and beyond. This exercise isn't just about dreaming — it's about setting the stage for your transformation and building a foundation for a life filled with purpose, passion, and fulfillment.

To further solidify the vision you've created and bring your future self to life, I encourage you to practice the New You meditation available at WomenWakingUp.com. This powerful meditation will guide you in embodying the future you desire, helping you step into the woman you're becoming. By regularly engaging in this visualization, you'll align your energy with your future self, making it easier to take purposeful steps toward becoming the new you. Embrace this practice and watch as your new reality begins to unfold before you.

Your Midlife Mantra

Between choosing your main area of focus from the Wheel of Midlife, setting a goal with the STEP method, reigniting your superpowers, and designing the new you, you have accomplished quite a bit in the first four chapters. Kudos to you! All this writing and visualizing may seem like a lot of effort, but this hard work will pay off. And remember, you are worth it! Your future self is thanking you.

Now we are going to take everything you brilliantly created in the first step, Free Yourself, and put it together into one power-packed sentence: your very own Midlife Mantra. What is a mantra, anyway? Think of the classic tale of *The Little Engine That Could*, where the little blue engine victoriously pulls a train full of goodies over a steep mountain, repeating to herself, "I think I can, I think I can..." You too will have a motivating chant to get you over your steep mountain. This mantra will encompass your action step and goal from the STEP method in chapter 1, your superpowers from chapter 2, and your vision of the new you from this chapter. Ready to create your special Midlife Mantra? I think you can, I think you can!

Step 1: Action

Going back to the STEP method at the end of chapter 1 (p. 15), list your answer to question 11: the small action step to achieve your goal. For example, *walk twenty minutes every day*, *join a pottery class*, *apply for a job*, *hire a financial planner*.

____

Step 2: Superword

Referring back to your superhero in chapter 2, choose a superword used to describe your strengths and superpowers. For example, *resilient*, *loving*, *friendly*, *fearless*.

____

Step 3: Goal

Again going back to the STEP method in chapter 1 (p. 17), list your goal. For example, *lose five pounds, reignite my creativity, get a fulfilling job, pay off credit cards.*

____

Step 4: Feeling

We need to add some emotion and feeling to your goal to make it stick. List how you want to feel as a result of achieving your goal. How will this feed your heart and soul? For example, *joyous, harmonious, powerful, beautiful.*

____

Step 5. Write Your Midlife Mantra

Now it's time to put all the pieces together and create your own Midlife Mantra. For example, this is my Midlife Mantra as I write this book:

> I will (Step 1: Action) get up at 5 a.m. using my (Step 2: Superword) zesty personality to successfully (Step 3: Goal) write *Women Waking Up* and, in so doing, become a woman who feels (Step 4: Feeling) alive.

It's your turn! Fill in the blanks with your answers from above.

I will (Step 1: Action) ______________________________
_______ using my (Step 2: Superword) ______________
personality to successfully (Step 3: Goal) ______________
___________________________ and, in so doing, become
a woman who feels (Step 4: Feeling) ______________.

Congratulations on crafting your Midlife Mantra! As you read it aloud, take a moment to truly embrace the powerful energy it brings. Feel the excitement and determination of the new life you are creating, and let that energy permeate every part of your being. This mantra is more than just words — it's a declaration of your commitment to yourself and your future. By uniting your dreams, superpowers, and goals into this single powerful statement, you've taken a bold step toward becoming the woman you aspire to be. Let this mantra guide you, motivate you, and remind you every day of the vibrant, empowered life you are designing.

Coming Up

Now that you've laid the foundation for your new life through visualization and mantra creation, it's time to take your transformation to the next level. In the next chapter, we'll explore how to harness the power of your emotions to elevate your energy and reach higher states of consciousness. By understanding and utilizing the scale of emotions, you'll learn how to consciously shift your emotional state, enhance your well-being, and maintain the positive momentum you've created. Get ready to venture deep into the emotional landscape and discover how to keep your energy high as you continue on your journey of midlife greatness.

5

ELEVATE YOUR EMOTIONS

Happiness is when what you think, what you say, and what you do are in harmony.

— attributed to Mahatma Gandhi

It took a few weeks for me to settle into life in Chicago — long days filled with training at my new job and the seemingly endless task of unpacking boxes in my new apartment. Finally, as I reached the last box, something extraordinary happened. I pulled out a small urn containing my brother's ashes, and it struck me that the date was March 31st — my brother's birthday. Placing the little bronze urn, adorned with orange and yellow leaves trimmed in gold, on my dresser, I couldn't help but feel a wave of emotion wash over me.

This urn had quickly become more than just a resting place for his ashes; it became a symbol of all the sorrows I had buried deep within me. Not only the grief of losing my brother, but the weight of all the unprocessed losses from my past — losses I had never allowed myself to properly mourn. Grief has a peculiar way of creeping up on you, and when it does, it can be absolutely devastating.

I had heard the term *dark night of the soul* before, but I never truly understood its meaning — until it became my reality shortly after moving to Chicago. My dark night of the soul arrived during the first of countless lonely, sleepless nights that seemed to stretch on forever, amplifying the torment of my three familiar companions: depression, anxiety, and panic attacks. Haunting memories surfaced relentlessly — images of my ex-husband lying in his casket, the abuse I endured from a boyfriend, the struggles of being a pregnant teenager, the abandonment I faced as a child, and one traumatic event after another. These memories weren't just thoughts; they invaded my entire being, overwhelming my mind and body.

Despite my efforts to flip the switch on my negative thoughts and embrace the idea of becoming my own best friend, the deep emotional pain was inescapable. Feelings of shame, guilt, worry, anger, fear, despair, and sadness multiplied uncontrollably, like gremlins that fed on my suffering. Every sorrow I had tried to bury over the years resurfaced with a vengeance, refusing to be ignored any longer. There was no more pushing it down — my suffering had settled in and would remain until I confronted it head-on.

My breakthrough came when I realized something profound: My emotions weren't just happening *to* me — they were flowing *through* me. I began to see that emotions, while overwhelming, are also dynamic. They could shift and change if I chose to work with them rather than against them.

I discovered that I had the power to influence my emotional state by focusing on things that lifted my energy: gratitude, small moments of joy, and acts of kindness toward myself and others. I didn't have to be stuck in despair; I could slowly, intentionally move toward peace and even hope. This realization became a lifeline, showing me that while I couldn't change the past, I could change how I processed it in the present. The power was mine to reclaim.

The Emotional Thermometer

Think of your emotions like temperatures on a thermometer, ranging from cold to hot. At the bottom of the thermometer, you'll find the cooler, calming emotions — those that leave you feeling balanced and in control. These include feelings like:

- calmness
- love
- happiness
- gratitude
- hope
- peace
- compassion

As you move up the thermometer, the emotions get warmer and more intense, eventually reaching the hot zone where things start to feel overwhelming or out of control. These hotter emotions include:

- irritation
- frustration
- jealousy
- guilt
- anger
- resentment
- depression

Just as a physical thermometer measures your body temperature, your emotional thermometer reflects your internal state. When you're "cool," you're grounded and clearheaded, able to respond thoughtfully to situations. But when you're in the hot zone, you might feel reactive, overwhelmed, or out of balance.

Why All Emotions Matter

It's important to remember that *all* emotions — both positive and negative — play a vital role in your life. While cooler emotions often feel more pleasant and desirable, hotter emotions serve an equally important purpose. They are signals, guiding you to pay attention to what's happening inside and around you.

For example, emotions like fear and anger can help you recognize danger or set boundaries, while guilt can prompt you to make amends or improve your behavior. These "hot" emotions, though uncomfortable, are essential for survival, growth, and self-awareness. The goal isn't to avoid them but to learn from them and respond in healthy ways.

The Impact of Emotions on Your Life

Your emotional state doesn't exist in isolation — it affects your physical health, relationships, and overall well-being. Negative emotions like shame, guilt, grief, fear, and anger can manifest as physical symptoms or tendencies such as:

- depression
- social withdrawal
- sleep disorders
- muscle tension or atrophy
- high blood pressure
- digestive issues
- weakened immune function

Over time, unresolved emotional stress can lead to chronic health conditions. Beyond physical health, hot emotions can also influence other areas of your life:

- **Relationships:** Anger and shame can lead to frequent conflicts and misunderstandings, causing strain with loved ones.
- **Productivity:** Apathy and guilt can reduce motivation, leading to decreased focus and performance.
- **Coping mechanisms:** Persistent negative emotions might push you toward unhealthy behaviors, such as overeating or substance use.

- **Finances:** Fear and impulsive desires can lead to poor financial decisions, resulting in debt or instability.

From Struggle to Strength

The key isn't to avoid the hot zone entirely — it's to learn to recognize when your emotional temperature is rising and to respond with care. As with developing a fever when you're sick, experiencing hot emotions like anger or jealousy is a natural part of being human. These emotions are signals, not something to judge or fear. They remind you that something within you needs attention and care, whether through rest, reflection, or simply letting yourself feel and process the emotion.

Besides, life has a way of teaching us through both joy and hardship. While we all hope to avoid suffering, the truth is that pain and challenges are part of the human experience. In fact, they're necessary for growth. It's through facing difficult emotions — grief, anger, fear, and sadness — that we gain the strength, wisdom, and resilience to thrive.

Imagine living your life locked away in a castle, surrounded by everything you think you need to be happy — comfort, success, and security. At first, it might seem ideal, but over time, you'd start to feel trapped, disconnected from the world, and unfulfilled. To truly grow and evolve, you must step outside those walls and confront life as it is, embracing both the beauty and the pain.

This is what I realized during my journey. For years, I tried to numb my pain and avoid uncomfortable emotions, building walls to protect myself from the world. But those walls also kept me from experiencing joy, connection, and freedom. It wasn't until I began to fully acknowledge and understand my emotions that I was able to break free.

By stepping outside my self-imposed walls, I stopped being controlled by my emotions and started learning from them. I may not have reached enlightenment, but I've gone from living in a constant state of pain and suffering to creating a life filled with more love, peace, and joy. I am the queen of my own castle now — and you can be too.

ACE Your Emotions

My lovely queen, I want to share with you my three-step ACE method: *awareness*, *choice*, *engagement*. This approach will help you boost your emotional energy, your self-awareness, and your physical and mental well-being. By practicing this method, you'll learn to own your emotions instead of letting your emotions own you. Let's embark on this empowering journey together.

Step 1: Awareness

The first step to mastering your emotions is *becoming aware of your current emotional state*. Start by regularly checking in with yourself throughout the day and asking: *What emotion am I feeling right now?*

Are you experiencing cooler, calming emotions like tranquility, love, gratitude, or joy? Or are you feeling hotter, more intense emotions like anger, frustration, or jealousy? Whether you're feeling good, bad, happy, or sad, simply notice your emotions without judgment.

Acknowledging your emotions is a powerful act. It reminds you that all emotions — whether pleasant or uncomfortable — are part of the human experience. By identifying what you're feeling and naming it, you take the first step in understanding yourself more deeply and regaining control over your emotional energy.

Step 2: Choice

Once you are aware of your current emotional state, *you have the power to choose how you respond and consciously shift to higher states.* This doesn't mean avoiding or ignoring challenging emotions — it means recognizing when it's time to process, learn from, and ultimately move through them.

Set an intention by affirming your desire to shift toward a more balanced emotional state when the time feels right. For example, you might say to yourself, *I choose to release frustration and welcome calm*, or *I let go of fear and invite courage*. These affirmations act as a gentle reminder that you have control over your emotional energy.

Remember, there are times when staying in warmer emotional states is necessary for healing. For example, if you've experienced a significant loss, grief is a natural and essential emotion. Ignoring it might delay healing and cause unprocessed emotions to surface later in unhealthy ways. Similarly, if you feel guilt after an argument, reflecting on your actions can help you understand your triggers, make amends, and grow from the experience.

Uncomfortable emotions are not inherently bad — they serve a purpose. The key is to honor what they're teaching you and not stay in these states longer than necessary. Once you've acknowledged and worked through the emotion, choose to move toward more empowering states like peace, gratitude, or hope. This intentional shift allows you to find balance and keep moving forward on your journey to emotional well-being.

Step 3: Engagement

Engage in activities and practices that naturally elevate your emotional energy and promote higher states of consciousness, making them part of your daily routine. Here are a few activities that could help you during turbulent times:

- **Gratitude journaling:** Write down three things you are grateful for each day. Gratitude shifts your focus from what's lacking to what's abundant in your life.
- **Physical exercise:** Engage in regular physical activity, such

as walking, yoga, or dancing. Exercise releases endorphins, which boost your mood and energy level.

- **Meditation and deep breathing:** Practice meditation or deep breathing exercises to calm the mind and reduce stress. This helps you shift from fear or anger to peace and serenity.
- **Positive affirmations:** Repeat positive affirmations that align with higher states of consciousness. For example, *I am love*, *I am peaceful*, or *I am worthy*.
- **Connecting with loved ones:** Spend time with family and friends who uplift and support you. Positive social interactions can enhance feelings of love, joy, and acceptance.
- **Acts of kindness:** Perform random acts of kindness. Helping others can elevate your emotional state by fostering feelings of compassion and connection.

By following these three steps — *awareness*, *choice*, and *engagement* — you can effectively shift from hotter states of emotion and consciousness to cooler, more empowering states. This process not only enhances your emotional well-being but also promotes a more fulfilling and balanced life.

It certainly did for me. That little bronze urn that was once a symbol of sorrow soon became a symbol of serenity. By confronting my deep-seated fears, I allowed a courageous and peaceful woman to emerge from my dark night of the soul.

Coming Up

In the next chapter, you'll continue the process of lightening your emotional load by carving away everything in your life that isn't truly you. As you clear away the clutter, you'll revisit the vision you created in step 1, evaluating what is helping and what is hindering your growth into your new-and-improved self. You'll also learn practical strategies for letting go of anything that no longer serves you, freeing yourself to move forward with clarity and purpose.

6

CARVE AWAY THE CLUTTER

We must be willing to let go of the life we have planned, so as to have the life that is waiting for us.

— Joseph Campbell, *Reflections on the Art of Living: A Joseph Campbell Companion*

In those first few months living alone in Chicago, I spent a lot of time in introspection. As if I were watching a movie on the big screen, I replayed the story of my life, from childhood as sweet little Wendy who laughed, danced, and played to the now unhappy grown-up Wendy who cried, worked, and worried. What went wrong?

I saw how that happy little girl became buried beneath the rubble of traumatic events, toxic relationships, and unfulfilling jobs. Instead of standing up for herself against abuse, she tirelessly sought adoration from her abusers. To avoid abandonment and the feeling of being unloved, she perfected her skills as an approval-seeking, problem-solving, people-pleasing perfectionist. And if there was any hint that someone might leave her, she left first. *I'll show them*, she thought. Wendy kept running from one lousy relationship and situation to the next, hoping to stumble upon happiness, but instead she collapsed from exhaustion.

My heart ached for little Wendy. I wanted to hold that innocent girl in my arms and tell her how much I loved her. Suddenly, a wave of shame washed over me. *Why did I let this happen? Why did I strive to be everything to everyone else, but nothing to myself?*

The answers I had been seeking finally came to me. I realized that the common thread woven through all the decades of drama was my fear of abandonment. This pervasive fear was the cause of everything that had gone wrong in my life. But then came the big eureka moment that would save little Wendy and bring her back to life: What I feared most was being abandoned by others, but in reality, I had been abandoning myself. *Boom!* That was it. I had become my own greatest fear.

That wave of shame transformed into a wave of empowerment. I held that little girl in my arms and said, "It's okay, you can relax now. I will never abandon you again. I got you." It felt like someone had lit a fire under me, because I jumped up with a newfound mission to take charge of my life. The dog days were over. With my fiftieth birthday around the corner, I was determined to make the second half better than the first. I would no longer allow myself to be abused in toxic relationships, bored with unfulfilling jobs, or overwhelmed with stress. It was time for my true, authentic self to shine, and the only way to achieve that was by clearing away the garbage that was cluttering my internal landscape.

The same applies to you. To uncover and unleash your true self, you must clear away the obstacles holding you back.

Who or What Is Holding You Back?

Imagine you're staring at a massive rough block of stone. Unshaped and unpolished, it appears heavy and unremarkable at first glance. But beneath the surface lies the potential for something extraordinary: a masterpiece that only you can create.

To begin the process, you first need to look past the rough

exterior and envision what's hidden within: the extraordinary woman you envisioned in chapter 4 — the woman you truly aspire to be, not the one others expect you to be. Your greatest qualities lie hidden beneath the rough edges of the stone, under the weight of your fears, insecurities, negative thoughts, bad habits, limiting beliefs, crappy relationships, and traumatic experiences.

Whew! That's a huge burden of baggage to tackle! At first, you might feel overwhelmed, tempted to give up before you even start — but you won't do that this time. No more abandoning yourself. It's time to carve out your inner masterpiece from the rubble of life that has been weighing you down. It's time to set yourself free and reveal the extraordinary creation that is already within you.

Here's the beautiful part: You don't have to add anything new. Everything you need is already there. The process of transformation isn't about becoming someone else; it's about chipping away everything that isn't truly you. Blow by blow, piece by piece, you remove the layers that no longer serve you — self-doubt, toxic relationships, fear, and anything else that dims your light.

In this next journaling process, you'll take a good, hard look at all areas of your life and decide what's not in alignment with the woman you envisioned. It's a process of letting go, of releasing what no longer belongs, so you can uncover the truest and most radiant version of yourself.

Keep in mind that you are not only the sculptor but also the masterpiece within the sculpture. You are both the artist at work and the work of art. You hold the vision, and you hold the power to create it. Grab your chisel, and let's start shaping your masterpiece!

The Statue of You

In this journaling exercise, you will refer back to the eight categories in the Wheel of Midlife: Family, Finance, Health, Career, Friends, Love, Leisure, and Growth. By answering the following questions, you can identify what is holding you back in each area and take steps to align more closely with your true self. This will help you lighten your emotional load and move forward with confidence, clarity, and strength.

Family

- What relationships within your family bring disharmony or stress to your life?
- How can you establish healthier boundaries with family members?
- Are there any family responsibilities or roles that feel burdensome or unaligned with your true self?

Finance

- Do you have debt weighing you down?
- What financial beliefs or fears are holding you back from financial freedom?
- Are there unnecessary expenses or financial obligations that need to be reevaluated?

Health

- Which bad habits do you need to kick to the curb?
- What negative thoughts or stressors are impacting your well-being?
- How can you incorporate more self-care and healthy practices into your routine?

Career

- Is your career causing chronic stress and unhappiness?
- What aspects of your career feel unfulfilling or out of alignment with your true self?

- Are there professional relationships or environments that hinder your growth?

Friends

- Which relationships bring disharmony or negativity into your life?
- Are your friendships supportive and uplifting?
- Do you feel valued and appreciated by your friends?

Love

- Is your romantic relationship supportive of your growth and happiness?
- Are there patterns in your love life that need to change?
- Does your partner encourage and appreciate the true you?

Leisure

- Are your leisure activities fulfilling and rejuvenating?
- Do you make enough time for hobbies and activities you enjoy?
- Are there any leisure activities that feel more like obligations than pleasures?

Growth

- Are you investing time in your personal development and growth?
- What negative thoughts and limiting beliefs need to go by the wayside?
- What habits or routines are hindering your personal and spiritual growth?

What Weighs You Down the Most?

- What are the top three things in your life that need to be carved away? Why?

I hope you had some *aha!* moments during the journaling process and are ready to start carving away! If you feel guilty for allowing yourself to reach this point in your life, give yourself grace. Hold that sweet little girl within you and tell her, "It's okay, you can relax now. I will never abandon you again. I've got you." Elevate those shameful emotions to a level of acceptance by letting go of judgment and finding peace in the present moment.

You may also feel overwhelmed as you stand before that gigantic block of marble. It will take time to chip away at that big boulder, but it is so worth it. *You* are worth it! Blow by blow, piece by piece, you will make it happen and uncover the truest version of yourself. As you move through your days, be mindful of what no longer serves you. Ask yourself, *Is this good or bad for me? Does this free me or bury me? Does this help me or hurt me?* Keep shaping your masterpiece, removing what weighs you down, and revealing the incredible woman within.

Coming Up

In the next chapter, you'll be introduced to the Lotus Effect, a powerful four-step subconscious release technique designed to help you transform midlife crises into opportunities for growth. Just as a lotus flower rises from the mud to bloom, you'll learn how to embrace the challenges of midlife — your "midlife mud" — and use them as fertile ground for your personal awakening. This chapter will guide you through the process of releasing old patterns and embracing your inner strength, so you can blossom into the next best version of yourself with grace and resilience.

7

CHOOSE TO BE AWAKENED

You never know how strong you are until being strong is your only choice.

— attributed to Bob Marley

As I mentioned earlier, I spent countless hours in introspection during those dark, lonely nights, replaying the story of my life. Two particularly life-altering scenes kept looping in my mind.

The First Life-Altering Scene

The first occurred on August 13, 2000. It was a typical Sunday morning filled with making pancakes, cleaning the kitchen, and getting myself ready for church while helping my two-year-old son get ready to be picked up by his dad for the day. Jason and I had been divorced for almost a year by then. Our marriage had been swift, both in its beginning and its end — a matrimony made in Vegas. The greatest gift from our brief union was the birth of our son, the cutest little blond chunky monkey on the planet.

Jason was supposed to arrive by 8 o'clock. As I hurried around the house picking up toys, I kept glancing at the clock on the wall, growing more frustrated with each passing minute.

8:10 a.m.: *Hmmm. That's strange. He's always on time.*
8:20 a.m.: *Errr. I'm going to be late for church!*
8:30 a.m.: *What the heck! He must have gone out with his friends last night.*

I kept texting his phone, but there was no response. *I'm sure he's just asleep.* My son sat on the edge of his bed, staring out the window, wearing his Mickey Mouse backpack filled with Matchbox cars, ready to show his dad. In his cute toddler voice, he asked, "Hey, Mom, when is Dad gonna be here?"

"Very soon. I'm sure he's getting gas or something."

I remembered that Jason had a landline phone at his new place, where he was renting a room from an elderly woman. I had only called there once before and couldn't quite remember the phone number. Was it 764-8902, 764-9802, or maybe 764-8920? The hands on the clock kept moving, and my anxiety was starting to build. *Something is wrong.* Frantically, I started dialing different combinations of numbers, only to hear the frustrating "Beeep — Your call cannot be completed" after every attempt.

Finally, the phone started ringing. I anxiously waited for someone to answer. A very shaky, out-of-breath woman's voice said, "Hello."

"Hi. Umm. I don't know if I'm calling the right number, but I'm looking for Jason."

Without hesitation, the woman shouted, "He's dead!"

My immediate response was "I'm sorry. I must've dialed the wrong number. I'm looking for Jason." In that moment, someone grabbed the phone from the woman, and I heard, "Ma'am, this is Officer Johnson. Jason was found curled up in his bed this morning with his alarm going off, but he never woke up. I'm sorry. Jason has passed away."

This can't be happening. This isn't real. How does a healthy twenty-six-year-old man die in his sleep? This is a question that will, unfortunately, always remain unanswered. According to the autopsy, his heart simply stopped beating. I had never been in more shock than at that moment. The shock was nothing compared to the pain of having to tell my sweet little boy that his dad wasn't coming to pick him up today. Or any day.

Needless to say, the aftermath of that horrifying moment continued for years. It wasn't just the difficulty of the unanswered questions, but the unresolved grief. As a single mom of two young boys working three jobs to make ends meet, I never gave myself the chance to grieve. It was always go, go, go. I had to be a strong woman and mother, so stopping to cry was not an option. I shoved every tear and fear so deeply down into my soul that they disappeared. Or so I thought.

The Second Life-Altering Scene

Fast-forward the movie of my life to July 6, 2018. The only sounds I could hear were the constant beeping of machines and my brother Bryan's labored breathing. It was early morning, the hospital room was cold, the lights were dim, and it was just the two of us. Sitting in a white plastic chair, holding Bryan's hand, I read aloud to him from *Jonathan Livingston Seagull* by Richard Bach. Occasionally, I glanced over the top of the book and saw his chest rise and fall as he struggled to breathe.

With tears streaming down my face, I continued reading, "You have the freedom to be yourself, your true self, here and now, and nothing can stand in your way." I wondered, *Can he even hear me? I hope these words are healing.*

It was the seventh day of my brother's coma. I wish I could say Bryan had only been suffering for those past seven days, but he had been struggling with addiction for more than thirty years. Despite his efforts to build a successful career, a beautiful family, and a nice house in the suburbs, addiction had taken over his life.

I was angry that I couldn't save him. Bryan had spent most of his life fighting his addictions, and I had spent most of mine fighting him about them. The fight was over, and the dreadful moment had arrived. I read one final sentence from the book: "Overcome space, and all we have left is Here. Overcome time, and all we have left is Now."

I kissed him on the forehead and whispered softly, "I love you. I set you free." I signaled to the doctors and nurses that it was time. With our family surrounding his bedside, the doctor pulled the plug, and the machines fell silent. With one hand on my mom's back, I felt her heart beating rapidly, sharing the pain of watching her son pass away. My other hand rested on my brother's chest, feeling his last heartbeat.

Wisdom in the Woes

My brother's death was the final straw that broke my back. I was already grappling with a divorce, battling Lyme disease and black mold toxicity, and enduring depression. Now I was left traumatized from witnessing my brother's death. Not to mention, all the years of suppressed tears and fears from Jason's death resurfaced.

After endlessly replaying these horrific scenes in my mind to the point of nausea, I decided to flip the script and seek the wisdom in the woes. Instead of solely focusing inward through self-reflection, I chose to channel that introspection into self-motivation. I used my past to propel me forward. I pondered the following questions to arrive at deeper understanding and personal growth:

- What lessons can I learn from the lives of Jason and Bryan?
- How can I use their experiences to grow and become stronger?
- What parts of their struggles mirror my own, and how can I address them?

- What can their journeys teach me about resilience and forgiveness?
- How can I honor their memories by making positive changes in my own life?
- What inner strengths can I uncover through their stories?
- How can I transform my pain into purpose and healing?

Little did I know that Jason's and Bryan's deaths would ultimately save my life. The darkness of their passing illuminated my own path. This newfound appreciation for those dark times inspired me to delve deeper into finding wisdom within the woes. I carefully unraveled the threads of the relationships that had broken my heart, the illnesses that were ravaging my body, and the various circumstances that had gone awry.

It all came down to perspective and my personal evaluation of past, present, and future scenes in my life — just as it does for everyone. Our every response or reaction in life is a choice, including whether we experience a midlife crisis or a midlife awakening, a breakdown or a breakthrough. We hold the power to turn a crisis into an opportunity, to shed light on the dark.

The Lotus Effect is a four-step subconscious release technique designed to help you transform your midlife crisis into an appreciation for the "mud" of midlife and use it to allow your new life to blossom. Let's bloom!

The Lotus Flower

I've always been fascinated by the lotus flower. At first glance, it appears to be just a delicate, pretty flower floating on the pond, soaking up the sunlight. But au contraire — the lotus is a power flower!

Every evening, the lotus retreats beneath the surface of the pond into the chilly, murky mud. It rests and sleeps there peacefully. Then every morning it pushes through the heavy mud and rises to the surface to greet the sun. As the sun's rays grow brighter and warmer, the lotus expands and opens its petals.

What is truly fascinating is that the petals of the lotus remain completely flawless, with no trace of mud. This phenomenon even has a scientific name: the lotus effect. As the lotus emerges, water droplets pick up the dirt, causing the mud to roll right off the petals.

As the sun sets, the lotus begins to close its petals tightly. It slowly dips back into the cold, dark mud, where it rests for the night. The next day, it repeats the cycle all over again.

Sink underwater, sleep in the mud, seek the sun, soak up the light.

The Lotus and You

To apply the story of the lotus to our own lives, let's examine what each element represents. The mud symbolizes the challenges and hardships we face. They include trauma, divorce, anxiety, death, disease, physical abuse, mental abuse, depression, debt, toxic relationships, bankruptcy, crappy jobs, unemployment, difficult childhoods, and addiction. That's one messy mud pie!

Though the mud represents negativity and darkness, it also brings positivity and nourishment. Just as the mud provides essential nutrients for the lotus's growth, our life experiences help us evolve and grow.

The reality is, we all have mud. We all endure cold, dark experiences. As the saying goes, "Shit happens." Mud happens. It's part of life. We just have to manage our mud. We need to appreciate the mud, just as the lotus appreciates the mud.

If the mud represents the darkness and fear in your life, then the sun represents the light and love. Just as the lotus depends on the sun to rise each day, you can rely on love to be present in your life every day. Fear and darkness are part of life, but so are love and light. It is the dichotomy and duality of existence. Every day when you rise, you have a choice of what to focus on: love or fear. The choice is yours.

In conclusion, mud is guaranteed in life. The key is not to carry the mud on your petals, as it will only weigh you down and hinder your growth. The solution lies in applying the Lotus Effect to your hardships, allowing you to blossom into the woman you were meant to be. By finding the wisdom in your woes, you can be *in* the world, but not *of* the world; *in* the mud, but not *of* the mud. Much like a lotus emerging from the cold, dark mud every morning, you can shake off your hardships and awaken to the light of a new you.

The Lotus Effect

Step 1: Sink

The first step in the Lotus Effect is to *sink*. This involves sinking into the mud of your life — facing your fears, losses, and traumas head-on. Much like I had to spend time in introspection evaluating my hardships, you too must spend time looking back at those pivotal moments in your life to uncover the nuggets of wisdom hidden within. By sinking into your past, you allow yourself to process and understand the experiences that have shaped you.

Spend some dedicated time in self-reflection. This can be done through journaling, meditation, therapy, or any other method that resonates with you and promotes your healing.

Instructions for Self-Reflection

- **Journaling:** Set aside quiet time each day to write about your experiences, emotions, and thoughts. Let your writing flow without judgment. Reflect on significant events and explore how they have impacted you.
- **Meditation:** Find a peaceful place where you won't be disturbed. Close your eyes, take deep breaths, and allow your mind to revisit the pivotal moments in your life. Observe

your thoughts and feelings without trying to change them. Let the insights come naturally.
- **Therapy:** Consider speaking with a therapist or counselor who can guide you through the process of exploring your past. They can provide a safe space for you to express your emotions and help you find clarity and healing.

Questions for Self-Reflection

To discover the hidden treasures in your mud, ask yourself these questions:

- What are the most significant challenges and traumas I have faced in my life?
- How have these experiences shaped my beliefs, behaviors, and attitudes?
- How did I cope with these challenges at the time, and what coping mechanisms have I developed since?
- Are there any recurring themes or patterns in my life that stem from these pivotal moments?
- What unresolved emotions or issues do I need to address to move forward?
- How can I show compassion and forgiveness to myself for the ways I have handled past struggles?

By submerging yourself into your past and reflecting on these questions, you can begin to find the wisdom in your woes and use it to propel yourself toward a brighter, more empowered future.

Step 2: Sleep

The second step in the Lotus Effect is *sleep*, which means allowing yourself to rest from the intense self-reflection. Diving into the dark times of our lives is not easy. For me, revisiting and writing about the memories of Jason's and Bryan's deaths were incredibly challenging. It's important to give your heart time to recover from the pain that comes from reopening old wounds.

Instructions for Rest and Recovery

- **Set boundaries:** Limit the time you spend on self-reflection each day to avoid emotional burnout. Designate specific times for reflection and times for rest.
- **Engage in soothing activities:** Participate in activities that bring you comfort and relaxation, such as reading, taking baths, listening to calming music, or spending time in nature.
- **Practice self-compassion:** Be gentle with yourself during this process. Acknowledge that it's okay to take breaks and that healing is a journey, not a race.
- **Consciously relax:** Practice mindfulness techniques such as deep breathing, progressive muscle relaxation, or guided imagery to help calm your mind and body.
- **Connect with loved ones:** Spend time with supportive friends and family who can offer comfort and understanding. Sharing your feelings with trusted individuals can provide emotional relief.
- **Promote physical rest:** Allow your body to rest by engaging in gentle physical activities like yoga or stretching. Avoid strenuous activities that may add to your stress.
- **Prioritize sleep:** Ensure you get enough restorative sleep each night. Create a calming bedtime routine to help you unwind and prepare for restful sleep.

Questions for Reflection During Rest

- How do I feel after revisiting these challenging memories?
- What emotions have surfaced, and how can I acknowledge and accept them?
- What activities help me feel calm and nurtured?

By incorporating rest and recovery into your self-reflection journey, you allow your heart and mind the necessary time to heal. Remember, just as the lotus retreats into the mud to rest each night, you too must take time to rest and rejuvenate.

Step 3: Seek

After spending time reflecting on your hardships and resting from the aftereffects of their troubling wake, it's time to *seek* the light in your darkness. Don't expect the wisdom of your woes to just reveal itself to you. Much like the lotus pushing through the mud to reach the rays of the sun, you too must push through your mud to find your light. Reach for the light as if your life depends on it — because it does. Without uncovering the wisdom from those hardships, you deprive your soul of the nourishment it needs to grow.

Instructions for Seeking the Light

- **Set clear intentions:** Clearly define what you are seeking. Whether it's understanding, healing, or growth, be specific about your intentions.
- **Stay persistent:** Like the lotus pushing through the mud, be persistent in your quest for light. Understand that this process takes time and effort.
- **Look for patterns:** As you reflect, identify patterns and recurring themes in your experiences. These can offer valuable insights into your life's lessons.
- **Engage in self-discovery practices:** Continue journaling, meditating, or speaking with a therapist. These practices can help you delve deeper into your experiences and uncover hidden wisdom.
- **Stay open and receptive:** Be open to receiving insights from various sources, including books, conversations, and experiences. Wisdom can come from unexpected places.

- **Cultivate gratitude:** Focus on gratitude for the lessons you've learned from your hardships. Acknowledging the growth and strength you've gained can help shift your perspective.

Questions for Seeking Wisdom

- What positive outcomes or lessons have emerged from my past hardships?
- What strengths have I developed as a result of overcoming these challenges?
- What opportunities for growth and healing are present in my current struggles?
- How can I use my experiences to help and inspire others?

By actively seeking the light in your darkness, you nurture your soul and promote personal growth. Remember, just as the lotus reaches for the sun, you too must strive to find the wisdom and light in your life's experiences.

Step 4: Soak

As you rise above the surface of your mud with your perfectly clean, beautiful petals, *soak* up the beauty of the light. Pat yourself on the back for facing your fears and making self-love a priority. The beauty of understanding the dark times in your life is that you uncover what truly brings you joy. Like the drops of water on the lotus petals that help it shed mud, drops of joy in your life let you shed darkness and fear. Adding more love and joy will help you thwart any residual or forthcoming pain and sadness. This is the love that nourishes your soul. This is the love that allows you to rise above the mud, open your petals, and bask in the beauty of the light.

Ways to Add More Love, Joy, and Happiness

- **Practice gratitude:** Keep a gratitude journal and write down three things you are grateful for each day. Focusing on the positives can enhance your overall sense of happiness.
- **Cultivate treasured relationships:** Spend quality time with loved ones. Nurture your relationships with family and friends by sharing experiences, expressing appreciation, and offering support.
- **Engage in hobbies:** Dedicate time to activities you are passionate about, whether it's painting, gardening, reading, or playing a musical instrument. Hobbies can bring immense joy and fulfillment.
- **Prioritize self-care rituals:** Incorporate self-care into your daily routine. This can include taking relaxing baths, meditating, exercising, or treating yourself to something special.
- **Volunteer and give back:** Helping others can bring a profound sense of joy and purpose. Find opportunities to volunteer in your community or support causes you care about.
- **Practice mindfulness and meditation:** Mindfulness and meditation help you stay present and fully experience each moment. This can reduce stress and increase your sense of peace and contentment.
- **Celebrate achievements:** Take time to celebrate your accomplishments, no matter how small. Recognizing your progress can boost your self-esteem and motivation.
- **Use positive affirmations:** Positive affirmations reinforce your self-worth and encourage a positive mindset. Repeat them daily to build confidence and inner strength.
- **Explore nature:** Spend time outdoors and connect with nature. Activities like hiking, walking on the beach, or simply sitting in a park can rejuvenate your spirit.

- **Laugh and have fun:** Don't forget to laugh and have fun. Watch a comedy, play games, or engage in activities that make you smile and laugh.

Questions for Reflection

- What activities bring me the most joy and fulfillment?
- What relationships in my life bring me the most love and happiness?
- What self-care practices can I implement to take better care of myself?
- How can I spread love and positivity to those around me?

By soaking up the beauty of the light and incorporating more love, joy, and happiness into your life, you nourish your soul and maintain a sense of peace and contentment. Like the lotus basking in the sunlight, you too can thrive and flourish above the mud.

Coming Up

A wonderful way to add a drop of joy to your life and complete the second step to FREEDOM is by listening to the Reset Your Life meditation available in the FREEDOM Meditation Series at WomenWakingUp.com.

At this stage, your Wheel of Midlife is rolling big-time. And now it's time to make your dreams come true. In the next chapter, I'll walk you through a journaling and meditation exercise to help you envision, feel, and manifest your dreams — the same method I used to create my new life. During this exercise, you will learn the targeted steps that will take you from your current life to your dream life.

STEP

ENVISION A NEW FUTURE

8

MAP OUT YOUR MIDLIFE DREAM

Your vision will become clear only when you look into your own heart. Who looks outside, dreams; who looks inside, awakes.
— attributed to Carl Jung

During my midlife awakening, I knew that if I was going to become a new-and-improved Wendy behind the wheel of a brand-new motorhome cruising across the country, I had to get crystal clear on exactly what I wanted in every area of my life. I also knew that if I was going to put in the effort to change my life, I might as well go all out. If I was going to dream, then I was going to dream *big*.

I grabbed my journal, curled up on the couch with a fresh cup of coffee, and as fast as my glittery pink pen would go, I wrote in detail everything I wanted to create in the next chapter of my life. When I say *detail*, I mean down to the auto-leveling jacks on my 2022 Thor Delano 24FB with diesel engine, black full-body paint with blue and silver stripes, beige interior, cute navy accent pillows from Pottery Barn, and a moonroof so I could lie in the bed above the cab and watch the stars sparkle at night in the Sedona desert. That kind of detail.

I didn't stop there. With my Wheel of Midlife in mind, I went spoke by spoke and addressed each category of my life: Family, Finance, Health, Career, Friends, Love, Leisure, and Growth. I described my dream career of starting my own podcast on the road and becoming an author of a book to empower women in midlife. I wrote a list of the healthy foods I would eat and exciting daily activities to match this new energetic, confident, and strong woman that I would become.

Exhausted from hours of writing but exhilarated from the possibilities of a new life, I leaned back on the couch. The journal I was holding had once been filled with sad thoughts and dreadful days but now was bursting with happy thoughts and yummy dreams. I looked at a painting on my wall that said in big, bold letters *THOUGHTS BECOME THINGS*, and I thought to myself, *Well, if that's the case, then I need to make these dreams into things!*

And so I did. Now it's your turn.

Planting the Seeds of Your Dreams

If there is one chapter in this entire book that I want you to fully grasp the most, it's this one. This is where the magic happens. This is where you start to make that shift into a new life and a new you.

So far, you have been concentrating on one main category on your Wheel of Midlife and taking the necessary steps to improve that area. In this chapter, though, you will create your dream life according to all eight categories. I mean, why only manifest one-eighth of your dream life when you can create the whole kit and caboodle? The goal of this chapter is for you to envision your dream, believe in your dream, and trust that the universe will take care of the rest, because it will.

Dreams. Remember those? Dreams are those exciting things you used to imagine as a child that now seem so difficult to visualize as a grown-up. Why is that? What happened that made you stop dreaming? Life happened. You got busy raising kids, building a career, managing a household — and trying to juggle it all without losing your mind.

Not to mention that somewhere in the middle of the madness, you lost faith in dreaming. Your dreams may have been torn to shreds by all the nondreamers, judged by others as unrealistic or just plain silly, or simply forgotten altogether. After all the dream disappointments, you wonder if dreams can even come true for you. I am here to remind you that your dreams matter — and *you* matter.

At this point in the book, you've gotten your Wheel of Midlife rolling, empowered your superpower, become your own BFF, stepped into the new you, elevated your emotions, carved away your clutter, and kicked off your midlife awakening. All the work you have done thus far has been tending to the soil of your garden, and this chapter is where you will plant the seeds of your dreams.

Before I give you the steps to make your dream life come true, let's first define dreams and the purpose of dreaming: A dream is a strongly desired goal, a vision, a creation of the imagination. The purpose of dreaming is to create your reality and your life. Dreaming is essential for creating — no matter the size of the dream.

A dream is made up of thoughts, images, and emotions, all of which are conceived in that beautiful mind of yours. Thoughts become things, so whatever you create in your mind you can create in your life. As long as you are breathing, you are thinking — and therefore, you are creating. Whether you are conscious of your thoughts or not, those thoughts are manifesting your future. So make the choice to think big thoughts, dream big dreams, and create a big life.

Ready? Let's do it!

The Midlife Masterpiece Process

In this three-step exercise, I will guide you to decide on your dream life, add energy and feeling to your dream, and create your Midlife Masterpiece.

Step 1: Decide on Your Dream Life

Pull out your Wheel of Midlife from chapter 1 and envision what you would like to create in each category of your wheel. Following are some questions in each category to help you get into that dream state. I want to remind you that you can dream whatever you want, so do not hold back! It's your dream and it's your life.

Family

- What kind of relationships do you want to nurture with your loved ones, such as children, parents, siblings, or chosen family?
- How do you envision spending meaningful time with your family or close connections? More vacations, Sunday dinners, or fun outings?
- How would you like to celebrate holidays and special occasions with those who matter most to you?
- What traditions, new or old, would you like to create or continue with your family or close circle?
- How, and how often, do you want to communicate and stay connected with your loved ones?

Finance

- What is your financial dream life? To be debt-free? To reach a specific savings goal?
- What are some things you dream of purchasing or achieving with your financial freedom? A dream home? A once-in-a-lifetime trip? A creative project?
- Do you want to increase your income, start a side hustle, or explore a new career path?
- What kinds of investments or financial plans would you like to prioritize for your future?
- How do you envision managing your finances to feel secure, confident, and free?

Health

- What would you like to create for your health? What are your dreams for being in shape?
- What is your ideal body weight? How would you like to feel in your skin?
- How do you imagine your optimal eating and sleeping habits?
- What type of physical activities or sports do you want to incorporate into your routine?
- How do you plan to manage stress and maintain mental well-being?

Career

- What is your dream career? Do you wish you had your own business?
- Do you want a promotion? Dream of going back to college?
- What would you do if money wasn't an issue?
- What skills or expertise would you like to develop in your career?
- How do you envision balancing your work and personal life?

Friends

- What is your ideal friendship? What qualities do you value most in a friend?
- Do you dream of creating new friendships?
- How would you like to spend more quality time with your friends? Girls' trip? Start a book club? Monthly Zoom happy hour?
- How do you want to support and be supported by your friends?
- What fun activities or hobbies would you like to do with your friends?

Love

- What is your dream love life? What kind of relationship do you want to create?
- How would you like to spend time with your partner?
- What is your ideal sex life?
- How would you like to be as a partner?
- What shared goals and dreams do you have with your partner?
- How do you plan to nurture and grow your relationship over time?

Leisure

- What is on your bucket list that you want to check off? What fun things do you dream about doing? A trip to Greece? A dance class?
- How do you imagine more *me* time?
- What hobbies or interests do you want to pursue in your free time?
- What's your ideal way to relax and unwind after a busy day or week?
- What new experiences or adventures do you want to explore?

Growth

- What do you envision for more personal growth? Do you dream of having more time for meditation, reading, and journaling?
- Do you wish to attain more confidence and courage in your life?
- What personal development courses or workshops would you like to attend?
- How do you plan to overcome challenges and setbacks in your growth journey?

- What mentors or role models inspire you, and how can you learn from them?

Now it's time to start mapping your future dream life. By the end of this process, you will have eight little "dream seeds" ready to start manifesting. I want you to write about your dream life in as much detail as possible. And I mean detail! If you have a wishy-washy dream, you will get wishy-washy results. If you have a crystal-clear dream, you will get crystal-clear results. Simple as that. The more distinct and detailed your vision is, the more easily it will unfold for you.

For example, if your dream is to start your own business, describe your products and services, your customers, and your ideal day in your new business. If your dream is to find a loving partner in life, describe this amazing person, your beautiful relationship, and how you bring joy to each other. Don't worry about how you will make this dream come true, just write freely about what you want — uncensored and unlimited. Have fun with your dream!

You can use a notebook, journal, whiteboard, or even a blank piece of paper to capture your vision. Write it out as shown in the template below. And if you want extra guidance, the *Women Waking Up Playbook* is a great tool to help you organize your thoughts and bring your dreams to life. You can grab your copy at WomenWaking Up.com.

Write until you're fully immersed in your dream. Let it flow. When you make the dream a reality in your mind, you set the stage to make it a reality in your life.

For My Dream Life, I Will Create…

Family:

Finance:

Health:

Career:

Friends:

Love:

Leisure:

Growth:

You did it! You are a dream master. Now it's time to add some energy to your seeds.

Step 2: Add Energy and Feeling

As I mentioned previously, dreams are made up of thoughts, images, and emotions. So far, you have the image of what you want and your thoughts to support that image. Now you need the emotion to put your dream in motion! Emotion is "energy in motion." It's the energy that drives those thoughts and images to manifest in your life. Essentially, you have to *feel* your dream.

Now I will guide you through my Envision a New Future meditation where you will take those eight dream seeds and visualize your dream in such detail that it'll be as if you're actually living it. Spend at least fifteen minutes doing this. A recording of the Envision a New Future meditation is available at WomenWakingUp.com. If you listen to the recording, it is best to close your eyes to shut down your sense of sight and drop further into the meditation.

Envision a New Future Meditation

Sit in a comfortable position. Breathe naturally. Imagine a pot of soil in front of you, and your eight little seeds sitting in the palm of your left hand. You will plant one seed at a time.

Close your eyes, drop into your heart, and feel the emotions arise as you hold the seeds of your dream life in the palm of your hand. This is your opportunity to allow your imagination to run free. There is nothing off-limits — you deserve the very best that life has to offer. The beautiful life you desire is right here for your enjoyment.

*Starting with **Family**, imagine picking up the seed with your right hand and holding it over the pot of soil.* What is your ideal relationship with your family? What activities do you dream of doing together? Is there a relationship that needs more love and attention? With the vision of your dream still present in your mind, drop the seed into the imaginary pot of soil you picture in front of you. Your family dream has been planted and is ready to grow.

*Now it's time to pick up the next seed, the seed of **Finance**.* How do you envision being financially free? How much money do you want in savings? What would you like to buy in your future? A new home? A new car? A cruise around the world? With the vision of your dream still present in your mind, drop the seed into the imaginary pot of soil you picture in front of you. Your finance dream has been planted and is ready to grow.

*Now it's time to pick up the next seed, the seed of **Health**.* Visualize what you look and feel like in your dream body. What do you imagine eating and drinking every day? How do you sleep? How do you move and exercise your body? With the vision of your dream still present in your mind, drop the seed into the imaginary pot of soil you picture in front of you. Your health dream has been planted and is ready to grow.

*Now it's time to pick up the next seed, the seed of **Career**.* What do you imagine as a fulfilling career? What excites you? How would you like to succeed in your career? With the vision of your dream still present in your mind, drop the seed into the imaginary pot of soil you picture in front of you. Your career dream has been planted and is ready to grow.

Now it's time to pick up the next seed, the seed of ***Friends***. Which friends would you like to spend time with in your dream life? How would you like to spend time with those friends? More girls' nights out? A weekend trip? How would you like to feel in your friendships? With the vision of your dream still present in your mind, drop the seed into the imaginary pot of soil you picture in front of you. Your friendship dream has been planted and is ready to grow.

Now it's time to pick up the next seed, the seed of ***Love***. Who is your dream partner in life? What do they look like? How do they make you feel? How do you make your partner feel? What do you imagine doing together? Date nights? Vacations? Making dinner together? With the vision of your dream still present in your mind, drop the seed into the imaginary pot of soil you picture in front of you. Your love dream has been planted and is ready to grow.

Now it's time to pick up the next seed, the seed of ***Leisure***. What fun and fulfilling things do you imagine doing in your dream life? What new hobbies would you like to take up? How do you imagine spending more *me* time? Spa days? Walks in the park? Going to museums? With the vision of your dream still present in your mind, drop the seed into the imaginary pot of soil you picture in front of you. Your leisure dream has been planted and is ready to grow.

Finally, it's time to pick up the next seed, the seed of ***Growth***. How do you imagine growing and evolving? Reading more books? Listening to podcasts? Meditating? How will you feel as a new woman? Confident? Courageous? Calm? With the vision of your dream still present in your mind, drop the seed into the imaginary pot of soil you picture in front of you. Your growth dream has been planted and is ready to grow.

Boost Your Dreams with Affirmations

You've now mapped out all eight categories of your midlife dreams. Take a moment here to simply relax, breathe, and imagine your eight dream seeds. It's time to add some positive words of affirmation with the following mantras. This will help reinforce all the intention and energy you have already instilled.

Repeat out loud:

My dream life is mine for the choosing.
I am worthy and deserving of this wonderful new future I am designing.
I have faith that my seeds will grow.
My dreams are becoming reality.

Take in one more long, deep breath as you gently return to the present moment and reawaken to your surroundings.

Remember to be open to the limitless possibilities of the life you desire. As you rise above the things that previously held you down, do so with gratitude as you enter into the future you love, appreciate, and design. Embrace the now and move forward with confidence and determination.

Welcome to your new dream life that is already underway! This part of the process is where you need to believe beyond a shadow of a doubt that your dreams will come true. Believe in your dream, embody your dream, and become your dream.

Step 3: Create Your Midlife Masterpiece

Vision boards are so much fun! If you're not familiar with them, they're visual depictions of what you want to create in your life, and you make them by collaging pictures and words that represent all the things you want for yourself. Seeing your vision board every day helps to add that energy of excitement about your future to come. I create a new one every year to keep my dreams updated, and it helps me gain even more clarity on what I want to manifest for my future. On the next page, you'll find one of my vision boards — the one I created in 2021 to help me manifest my dream life. This board played a pivotal role in the transformation I share throughout this book.

The vision board that you will create aligns with the eight categories on the Wheel of Midlife, which is great because you have already journaled and meditated on what you want each category to look like in your future dream life. All you have to do now is take the vision in your mind and turn it into artwork for your wall. The sky's the limit when it comes to designing your vision board. Just like your life, your vision board is your masterpiece, and you can create whatever you want.

Wendy's own midlife vision board

If you would like to create a digital vision board, you can use my Canva template available at WomenWakingUp.com, or if you prefer to take a trip to the craft store, here are the basic materials you will need:

Poster board
Magazines

Scissors
Glue
Optional: Pens, markers, glitter, stickers, decorative tape, printed photos or inspiring words, scrapbook paper or colorful backgrounds, ribbons, gems, or other crafty embellishments

Spread the materials out on a table and divide the poster board into eight sections according to the Wheel of Midlife categories: Family, Finance, Health, Career, Friends, Love, Leisure, Growth.

Refer to the dream map that you wrote out earlier in this chapter. Clip or print out images and words that depict your dreams for each category.

Crank up the music and have some fun! Decorate your vision board with colors, glitter, whatever suits your fancy!

Hang up your vision board and look at it every day, or if you created a digital vision board, you can make it your computer wallpaper. As you look at your vision board, imagine these images as being your new reality. The more you believe, the more you will receive.

Coming Up

Now that you have created your Midlife Masterpiece, we are really going to turn up the dial of your midlife makeover. In the next chapter, I'll guide you to reconnect with and celebrate the body you live in! This chapter emphasizes the importance of loving, nourishing, and moving your body — midlife belly and all.

9

LOVE THE BODY YOU LIVE IN

I finally realized that being grateful to my body was key to giving more love to myself.

— Oprah Winfrey

I have great news! If you've been searching for the magic solution to flatten your tummy, perk up your breasts, and lift your tush, your search is over! You can stop wasting time on the latest fad diets, exercise gimmicks, or cosmetic crazes.

On average, women spend an astonishing seventeen years of their lives on diets. Considering the average lifespan of a woman in the United States is 80.2 years, this means women spend about 21 percent of their lives dieting. Besides the significant time commitment, women also spend a substantial amount of money trying to change their bodies. Annually, Americans spend over $90 billion on dieting and weight loss products, and that number is growing fast. Not to mention that women spent around $16.5 billion in 2018 on cosmetic plastic surgery and minimally invasive procedures, according to the American Society of Plastic Surgeons.

If we look at these staggering statistics differently, we might congratulate ourselves on our dedication. But dedicated to what, and why? When you're on your deathbed, I doubt you'll regret no longer fitting into your skinny jeans. What you will regret is spending a huge chunk of your life chasing an unrealistic ideal.

Plus, spending all this time and money seeking to "improve" our body image leads to high levels of stress and mental health issues. A study by the UK's Mental Health Foundation found that 40 percent of women reported feeling anxious and 45 percent reported feeling depressed because of their body image.

I understand that as women, we all want to feel sexy, desirable, and gorgeous, especially as we hit our midlife years when our bodies start to change — our breasts head south, our skin thins, and crow's feet appear. But at what cost? The reality is that aging is a natural process of the human body. Just like trees, flowers, and animals, our bodies are living organisms that will eventually decompose and return to the earth. Until you take your last breath, embrace the beauty of your body.

Despite the natural aging process, we can still reconnect with and celebrate the beauty of our bodies. Instead of pouring our time, money, and energy into trying to perfect them, what if we channeled those efforts into using our gifts, spreading joy, and fulfilling our purpose? Imagine the powerful and transformative women who would emerge from such a movement, and more importantly, the profound impact they would have on the world.

We need more trailblazers like Susan B. Anthony, who played a crucial role in the fight for women's right to vote; Ida B. Wells, who ensured that the voices of African American women were included in the fight for equal rights; Amelia Earhart, the first woman to fly solo nonstop across the Atlantic, symbolizing women's capabilities; and Rosa Parks, whose brave refusal to give up her bus seat in 1955 became a pivotal moment in the Civil Rights Movement. These women weren't obsessed with bathing suit season; they were too busy making a difference in the world. Their bodies were the vessels that carried them toward their purpose, enabling them to create lasting change. The same holds true for you.

The Vehicle of Your Soul

Pause for a moment and take a look at your body. What you see is a living, breathing organism filled with approximately 37.2 trillion cells, about 5 liters of blood, and 206 bones. All the parts of this beautiful body of yours work in harmony, allowing you to think, move, and experience life.

Consider the intricate network of veins and arteries that transport your blood, delivering oxygen and nutrients to every cell. Think about the strength and structure provided by your bones, supporting your movements and protecting your vital organs. Reflect on the muscles that contract and relax, enabling you to perform countless actions every day.

Marvel at your brain, the control center of your body, processing information, making decisions, and storing memories. Appreciate your skin, the largest organ, which shields you from external elements and helps regulate your body temperature.

Your every breath, every heartbeat, every thought, and every movement are a testament to the incredible complexity and resilience of your body. This miraculous system works tirelessly to keep you alive and thriving, often without you even noticing.

It's not so much what can be seen that is so astounding; it's what cannot be seen. It's the amazing soul merged with the one beautiful body you have been gifted in this lifetime. Your soul, filled with boundless potential, profound wisdom, and an endless capacity for love and growth, is what truly makes you extraordinary.

So the next time you look in the mirror, remember that your body is so much more than its outward appearance. It is a masterpiece of biological engineering, a manifestation of the wonders of life. Treat it with the care and respect it deserves.

Your body accomplishes a lot on its own, but it needs your help to function at its best. Providing it with water, oxygen, and nourishment is essential for survival. After all, your body is the vehicle that carries your precious soul through this lifetime. To let your spirit shine brightly, your body must be strong, healthy, and vibrant.

The ABC's of Health

While the human body is a marvel of complexity, taking care of it can be straightforward. In this chapter, we'll return to the fundamentals, which I call the ABC's of health: *awareness*, *basics*, and *conditioning*. By following the ABC's of health, you can adopt a balanced and mindful approach to taking care of your body, promoting both physical and mental well-being.

Awareness

Awareness involves being mindful and intentional in how you care for your body. In our fast-paced society, we often rush through our days, losing connection to both our bodies and souls. If you don't slow down, you might find yourself mindlessly scarfing down a piece of chocolate cake without even noticing. While such moments of inattentiveness may not cause immediate harm, over time, they can become a habit that leads to serious health issues, leaving your body in need of urgent care, much like a vehicle stranded on the side of the road.

That's exactly what happened to me. Overall, I maintained a healthy mindset about my body, and with over twenty years of experience in the healthcare industry, I had considerable knowledge about self-care. My diet and exercise routines were not perfect, but I ate my vegetables, drank plenty of water, and practiced yoga regularly. On the surface, it seemed I was doing everything right, yet internally, my body was breaking down. I began experiencing a wide range of symptoms — joint pain, poor sleep, migraines, skin rashes, nausea, diarrhea, blurred vision, fever, fatigue, numbness, shortness of breath, dizziness, confusion, nosebleeds, and intense night sweats. Although accidental and environmental factors played a role in my decline — black mold toxicity from a contaminated house, Lyme disease from a tick bite, and three herniated discs from a near-death car accident — the primary culprit behind my body's breakdown was the big *S*: stress.

Remember my unwelcome trio — depression, anxiety, and panic attacks? They did quite a number on me. They didn't just leave my vehicle on the side of the road, they nearly sent it over a cliff. The sleepless nights, chronic worrying, and persistent pain broke me down until I couldn't go any further. But then I had a revelation: Who was driving this vehicle carrying my soul through life? Was it me or this trio of troublemakers? Those troublemakers would have to get in the backseat because it was time for me to take the wheel.

All the dreams I wanted to manifest in my life wouldn't stand a chance if I couldn't stand strong in my own body. I needed a reliable, healthy body to drive me toward my dreams. Just as I'd decided to care for little Wendy who had been neglected, I made the choice to take care of my body, which had also been ignored for too long. This is when awareness became crucial to my healing and well-being. In addition to changing my thoughts, elevating my emotions, and carving away my clutter, I became more mindful of my daily actions. It was as if a drone was hovering over me 24-7, monitoring how I moved, ate, and slept. By observing my careless mistakes, mindless activities, and unhealthy habits, I was able to adjust my behaviors to align with the vibrant, purpose-driven Wendy I envisioned for my future.

With this newfound awareness, I realized that small, intentional changes could have a profound impact on my overall well-being. By imagining your own drone flying overhead around the clock, you can take some simple steps to cultivate awareness in your life. Awareness involves understanding and paying attention to the following:

- **How you start your day:** Begin your day with intention and positivity by creating a morning routine that sets the tone for the rest of your day. Do you incorporate activities like meditation, prayer, journaling, exercise, or planning?
- **How you eat:** Notice what you eat, when you eat, and how much you eat. Are you eating out of hunger, stress, or habit?

Do you rush through your meals, or do you slow down to enjoy the experience? Pay attention to how different foods make you feel. Do you feel bloated, achy, or sleepy after eating certain foods?

- **How you move:** Pay attention to your physical activity. Are you getting enough exercise? Do you sit for long periods? Does your body ache when you get out of the car or carry groceries?
- **How you think:** Be mindful of what you think and believe about your body. Practice positive self-talk and body positivity as you learned in chapter 3, "Become Your Own BFF."
- **How you behave:** Recognize patterns in your behavior that affect your health, such as sleep habits, hydration, and stress management.
- **How you end your day:** Consider your evening routines. Are you winding down in a way that promotes restful sleep and relaxation?

To deepen your awareness journey, take time to notate or journal about your observations. Reflect on each aspect of your day — how you start it; how you nourish yourself; how you move, think, and behave; and how you end your day. Writing down what you notice will help you identify patterns and areas that may need attention. By capturing these insights, you create a personalized roadmap for positive change. Journaling allows you to track progress and celebrate small victories, fostering a deeper connection with your body and mind. Your awareness is the key to unlocking lasting health and vitality — let your notes be the compass guiding you forward.

Basics

Basics refers to the foundational elements of a healthy diet and lifestyle. We are constantly bombarded with various opinions on how to nourish our bodies optimally, whether from social media, television, magazines, friends, family, or physicians. While incredible discoveries and advancements in healthcare have been made over the past few decades, the human body still requires its basic needs for survival: food, water, and oxygen. Human ingenuity will continue to drive innovation, but the fundamental requirements of our physical form remain unchanged.

Your body is a living, breathing organism. Poor lifestyle habits can steer your vehicle into a ditch, but healthy food will get you back on the road. Food is your fuel. Just as you wouldn't put subpar fuel in your car, don't do it to your body.

I follow the KISS principle when it comes to food: *keep it simple, sweetie*. It's not rocket science; it's just about going back to the basics. Being part of nature means we should consume as much as possible from natural sources. This doesn't mean you need to become vegan and live off the land, but it does mean focusing on a plant-based diet that emphasizes whole, unprocessed foods. Here are the basic guidelines that will keep your body running at its best.

Key Principles of Healthy Eating

- **Plant-based focus:** Prioritize a diet rich in vegetables, fruits, whole grains, legumes, nuts, and seeds. These foods should make up the majority of your meals. Aim for dishes like a colorful stir-fry with broccoli, bell peppers, and quinoa or a hearty lentil soup with a side of mixed greens. While animal products can still be included, they should take a backseat, acting as a complement rather than the star of your plate. For instance, a small portion of grilled salmon can accompany a generous serving of roasted vegetables.
- **Whole foods:** Emphasize foods that are as close to their natural state as possible. Opt for whole fruits instead of fruit juices, whole grains like brown rice or oats instead of refined grains like white bread or boxed mac and cheese,

and nuts or seeds instead of processed snacks. By choosing foods with minimal processing, you avoid hidden sugars, unhealthy fats, and artificial additives. For example, enjoy a breakfast of steel-cut oats topped with fresh berries and almonds, rather than a sugary cereal.

- **Legumes:** Beans, lentils, chickpeas, and other legumes are powerhouse ingredients, offering plant-based protein, fiber, and essential nutrients. Incorporate them into your meals as a primary protein source. You might enjoy a chickpea salad with a tahini dressing or a bowl of black bean chili with a side of avocado.
- **Moderate alcohol consumption:** If you choose to drink alcohol, do so in moderation, and preferably with meals. A glass of red wine enjoyed with dinner can be part of a balanced approach to health, aligning with many traditional diets that emphasize moderation.
- **Small portions of meat:** When including meat in your diet, opt for smaller portions, and think of it as an occasional treat rather than a daily necessity. For example, a small serving of roasted chicken can be part of a meal centered around whole grains and vegetables, like a farro salad with kale and roasted carrots.
- **Dairy:** Dairy should be consumed sparingly, with a preference for fermented options like yogurt, which support gut health. For a satisfying snack or breakfast, consider eating fruit and nuts atop plain Greek yogurt, rather than sugary, flavored varieties.
- **Healthy fats:** Choose fats that nourish your body, such as those found in olive oil, avocados, nuts, and seeds. These fats support heart health and add flavor to your meals. Drizzle extra-virgin olive oil over a salad of mixed greens, or snack on a handful of walnuts.
- **Whole grains:** Whole grains like quinoa, barley, farro, and brown rice should be staples in your diet. These grains

provide essential fiber, vitamins, and minerals. Swap out refined pasta for whole-grain alternatives, or make a satisfying grain bowl with a variety of vegetables and a light dressing.

- **Herbs and spices:** Use herbs and spices to add flavor and health benefits to your meals, reducing the need for added salt, sugar, or unhealthy sauces. Fresh herbs like basil, cilantro, and parsley can brighten up a dish, while spices like turmeric, cumin, and cinnamon can add depth and warmth. For instance, a simple grilled vegetable dish can be transformed with a sprinkle of fresh rosemary and a squeeze of lemon.
- **Hydration:** Just as important as the food you consume is the water you drink. Proper hydration is essential for every function in your body, from digestion and circulation to temperature regulation and joint lubrication. A good rule of thumb is to drink half your body weight in ounces of water each day. For example, if you weigh 150 pounds, aim for about 75 ounces of water daily. To make it simple, carry a reusable water bottle with you and refill it throughout the day. Your needs may increase if you're active, in a hot climate, or consuming diuretics like caffeine or alcohol.

Remember, the goal is to simplify your choices by focusing on these basic principles. When in doubt, head straight to the produce section and choose what nature offers in abundance. By keeping it simple and sticking to these basics, you'll be well on your way to nourishing your body with what it truly needs. With *awareness* and *basics* in place, you're ready to add *conditioning* to your routine, creating a balanced and healthy lifestyle that supports your well-being.

Conditioning

One of the most fascinating insights about longevity comes from Dan Buettner's research on the Blue Zones and his Power 9 principles, which highlight the lifestyle habits of the world's healthiest, longest-lived people, and it applies to our *C*, *conditioning*. As explained on the Blue Zones website, "The world's longest-lived people don't pump iron, run marathons, or join gyms. Instead, they live in environments that constantly nudge them into moving without thinking about it. They grow gardens and don't have mechanical conveniences for house and yard work."

So what I mean by *conditioning* isn't starting a routine to become Iron Woman. Conditioning involves taking deliberate actions to maintain and improve your physical fitness. It doesn't mean pushing yourself to the brink to achieve rock-hard abs and buns of steel. Rather, conditioning is about nourishing the living, breathing organism that graciously carries you through each day. Think of conditioning like hair conditioner: Just as conditioner lubricates and strengthens your hair, physical activity lubricates your joints, organs, muscles, and all the cells in your body. Without proper conditioning, your body can become stiff, brittle, and prone to breakdowns. By regularly moving your body, you provide it with the conditioning it needs to function as a well-oiled, strong, and resilient vehicle. Remember, motion is lotion!

Continuing with the KISS principle, let's keep your conditioning simple and effective. If joining a gym motivates you and keeps you active, that's fantastic. However, conditioning your body doesn't have to involve a gym membership or complicated routines. Returning to basics with activities like walking, stretching, and light exercises can be incredibly effective and accessible.

Walking is one of the easiest and most beneficial forms of exercise. It requires no special equipment and offers a range of health benefits, from enhancing cardiovascular health to elevating your mood. Even short bursts of walking can make a difference. Recent studies show that as little as ten minutes of walking (for example, before or after meals) can improve heart health, lower stress levels, and boost energy. Stretching is equally important, as it maintains muscle flexibility, strength, and overall joint health, helping you stay limber and agile. Light exercises, such as yoga or Pilates, can further improve your core strength, balance, and body awareness.

Let's not forget one of my favorite forms of exercise — dancing! If dancing is your thing too, then you'll absolutely love my Spotify playlist, "Women Waking Up: Beats to Ignite Your Soul," available at WomenWakingUp.com. This playlist is curated to spark your inner fire, celebrate your strength, and awaken your badass self, making every dance session an empowering experience.

The key to success is consistency and choosing activities that genuinely bring you joy, making it easier to stick with your routine. Remember, the goal of conditioning your body is to enhance your life and well-being, not to create additional stress. Keep it simple and enjoyable — something you eagerly look forward to each day.

Pressing Play on the 'Pause

As many of us women navigate perimenopause and menopause during our midlife years, incorporating more movement into our daily routine can be incredibly beneficial. Regular physical activity can significantly alleviate symptoms associated with this transition. Here are some key benefits:

- **Reduced hot flashes and night sweats:** Regular exercise helps regulate the body's temperature-control mechanisms, potentially reducing the frequency and severity of hot flashes and night sweats.
- **Improved mood and reduced anxiety:** Exercise stimulates the production of endorphins, the body's natural mood elevators. This can help combat mood swings, anxiety, and depression, which are common during menopause.
- **Better sleep:** Physical activity can improve sleep quality and help with the insomnia that can come with menopause.

Exercise helps regulate the body's circadian rhythms, promoting deeper and more restful sleep.

- **Weight management:** Menopause can lead to weight gain, particularly around the abdomen. Regular movement helps maintain a healthy weight, reducing the risk of obesity-related conditions such as heart disease and diabetes.
- **Stronger bones:** Weight-bearing exercises, like walking, running, and strength training, help maintain bone density and reduce the risk of osteoporosis, which becomes more prevalent with menopause.
- **Higher energy levels:** Regular exercise enhances overall energy levels and combats fatigue, making daily activities easier and more enjoyable.
- **Improved cardiovascular health:** Regular aerobic exercise improves heart health by lowering blood pressure, improving cholesterol levels, and enhancing circulation.
- **Enhanced cognitive function:** Exercise has been shown to improve memory, concentration, and overall cognitive function, helping to counteract the cognitive decline sometimes associated with menopause.
- **Reduced joint pain and stiffness:** Regular movement keeps joints flexible and muscles strong, reducing the risk of arthritis and alleviating the joint pain and stiffness that can accompany menopause.
- **Increased libido and sexual health:** Exercise improves blood flow and energy levels. This can enhance libido and sexual function, which are often affected during menopause.

As someone who is past menopause and has experienced hot flashes, achy joints, and mood swings, I can attest that incorporating regular physical activity into your daily routine can effectively manage many of the symptoms associated with perimenopause and menopause. This leads to a healthier and more comfortable transition through these life stages.

Comfort is the key word here. As you age beyond your midlife years into your seventies and eighties, you want to feel at ease in your body. You want the ability to play with your grandkids, travel the world, or enjoy a leisurely walk in the park. By being proactive and taking the necessary steps toward a healthier body during your midlife years, you are setting yourself up for a healthier and more vibrant body in your later years. Your ninety-year-old self will thank you for the effort you put in now.

ABC Wellness Plan

Incorporating wellness into your daily life doesn't have to be overwhelming or complicated. A simple and effective tool I recommend for starting your wellness journey is creating your own ABC Wellness Plan. By focusing on *awareness*, *basics*, and *conditioning*, you can create a strong foundation for a vibrant and healthy life as you navigate midlife and beyond. Here are some reflective questions to help you integrate these principles into your routine. Write your answers in your journal, and then commit to putting your ABC Wellness Plan into action starting tomorrow.

Awareness

- How will I bring more mindfulness to my daily routine?

Reflect on how you can become more aware of your body, mind, and habits. What small changes can you make to improve how you start your day, what you eat, how you move, and how you wind down?

Basics

- How will I nourish my body with the basics?

Consider how you can simplify your food choices by focusing

on whole, plant-based, and natural foods. What shifts can you make in your diet to prioritize better nutrition?

Conditioning

- How will I move my body and stay active?

  Think about how you can add more movement to your day, even in small ways. What types of physical activities bring you joy and are easy to fit into your schedule?

The ABC Wellness Plan will serve as a practical guide, helping you integrate wellness into your life in a manageable way, ensuring you feel empowered, healthy, and strong through midlife and beyond.

Coming Up

In the next chapter, you will embark on the fourth step to FREEDOM, where you get to embrace and explore. You'll learn techniques to drop your perfectionism, make mistakes, try new things, and simplify the process of reinventing yourself one step at a time. Embrace this journey with curiosity and openness as you continue to evolve and thrive.

STEP

EMBRACE AND EXPLORE

10

MAKE LITTLE CHANGES FOR BIG RESULTS

The future belongs to those who believe in the beauty of their dreams.

— Eleanor Roosevelt, *You Learn by Living: Eleven Keys for a More Fulfilling Life*

As I continued to chisel away at the heavy marble of my fears, I began to experience a transformation — my mind became clearer, my body healthier, and my spirit brighter. The light at the end of the tunnel was finally coming into view. Beneath the many layers of trauma was someone who had always aspired to be one of the trailblazing, badass women of the world. As the excess fell away, my true self began to take shape, along with a calling that had been waiting to be discovered.

Reinventing myself led to a profound discovery of my life purpose: helping women around the world overcome their struggles, wake up from their midlife comas, and design lives they love. I realized that if I could transform my life, I could guide others to do the same. However, just as I was beginning to embrace this new purpose, I encountered another roadblock.

My job in Chicago, while financially rewarding, constrained

my gifts and talents, keeping me from fully expressing my true potential. Additionally, the job could not be done remotely, which further limited my freedom and potential.

While I was making tremendous progress in improving my well-being and seeing the satisfaction scores on my Wheel of Midlife rise, I knew I had to break through this barrier to achieve my dreams. The answer to my problem came to me in an unexpected *aha!* moment, sparked by none other than a pair of black Valentino high heel shoes with skinny leather straps trimmed in gold studs. God rest their sexy little souls.

On a chilly, gray Chicago morning in the dead of winter, I was sitting on a velvet brown ottoman in my bedroom, slipping on my sexy yet very uncomfortable high heels for work. As I looked up, I noticed my vision board staring back at me from the wall above my dresser. Normally, I was the one staring at my vision board, but this time it seemed to be glaring at me as if to say, "Come on, Wendy! Let's make this RV dream come true! I'm not just a pretty picture, ya' know?"

As I fastened the strap of my high heel through the little gold buckle, I said aloud, "I hate wearing high heels! I want flip-flops, sunshine, and the keys to my RV!"

In that moment, as my vision board and I had our intense staredown, I realized that my dreams weren't just going to happen on their own; I needed to make them happen. But how was I going to do that? The same way I had gone from feeling utterly lost in Virginia to sitting on the ottoman in Illinois: by taking deliberate action and making intentional changes. It was time to kick my growth into gear and elevate my pursuit of my future goals.

This required some serious brainstorming. I looked at all eight categories of my life on my vision board: Family, Finance, Health, Career, Friends, Love, Leisure, and Growth. Grabbing a pen and my well-worn journal, I began making a to-do list of everything that needed to happen in each category to get me from where I was currently in my life to where I wanted to be — launching my new podcast from the dinette table of my brand-new RV.

Wendy's To-Do List

- **Family:** Share my future plans with my family. Chat with family members about their experience owning an RV to gather valuable insights and advice.
- **Finance:** Achieve record-breaking sales in my job to increase my income. Pay off debt and save up enough money for an RV down payment and one year of living expenses. Sell my car. Sell or donate furniture and belongings to raise additional funds. Cut back on dining out and shopping to save more money.
- **Health:** Order from a plant-based meal kit company to encourage cooking healthy meals at home, allowing for more relaxing evenings and better sleep. Incorporate more yoga into my workouts to support a healthy mind, body, and spirit. Complete EMDR (eye movement desensitization and reprocessing) therapy sessions to alleviate the distress associated with my traumatic memories.
- **Career:** Aim to become the top sales consultant of the year to reach my financial goals. Apply for a corporation license for my new podcasting and coaching company and open a business checking account. Hire a business coach to help design my podcast and business strategy. Engage a website designer, photographer for brand photos, and podcast editor. Research top podcasts and read books related to creating a successful online business to stay informed and inspired.
- **Friends:** Meet new friends online who live full-time in a motorhome to build a supportive community. Share my dreams with existing friends to gain their support and ideas.
- **Love:** Focus on improving my emotional well-being and

healing from toxic relationships to invite a loving partner into my future dream life.

- **Leisure:** Read books on how to live full-time in an RV and plan out my road trip. Map out the details of my dream RV setup — inside and out. Purchase a bike and bike rack for the back of my RV. Shop for essential items like bedding, an outdoor grill, and camping supplies.
- **Growth:** Practice self-care routines such as taking warm baths before bed and scheduling weekly massages to manage stress from the extra work. Listen to self-help audiobooks during my long commutes to work to continually learn and grow. Meditate every morning and evening to maintain inner peace and clarity.

When I first wrote out my extensive to-do list, it felt overwhelming, but it was also incredibly exciting! I could almost taste the juicy burger cooked on my shiny red Coleman grill and feel the warmth of the desert sun on my face as I sat in my comfy camping chair. To make this dream a reality, I needed to identify the subtle shifts in my daily habits that would create quantum leaps in my life. Instead of spending my free time goofing around sipping martinis with my girlfriends or binge-watching the latest series on Netflix, I resolved to use that time more wisely.

For the next year, I continued selling homes during the day while dedicating my nights and weekends to designing my dream career. I spent countless hours planning, sharing, and writing, steadily crafting a new path for myself. With the keys to my new life dangling in front of me, I went from making zero dollars to earning half a million dollars in less than two years. The mountain of debt that had weighed me down for so long disappeared, and my savings account finally had a balance — just what I needed to buy my dream RV. Eventually, I knew it was time to take the show on the road. I was ready to launch both the new podcast and the new me out on the open road and fulfill my dreams.

Now it's time to put your dreams into overdrive with the Quantum Leap method, a powerful approach to turning your aspirations into reality.

 The Quantum Leap Method

Achieving big dreams doesn't always require massive leaps; often, it's the subtle shifts in daily habits that create the most significant changes. By breaking down your goals into manageable steps and making intentional changes, you can create quantum leaps in your life. Here's how.

Step 1: Evaluate Your Life Categories

Start by looking at all eight categories of your life: Family, Finance, Health, Career, Friends, Love, Leisure, and Growth. Assess where you currently stand in each category and where you want to be.

Step 2: Make a Detailed To-Do List

Write down all the steps you need to take in each category to move from where you are now to where you want to be. Be specific and thorough — whether it's saving money, improving your health, or enhancing your career skills, every step matters. Use your journal or the *Women Waking Up Playbook* to jot down your actionable steps and create a roadmap to your dreams. Let your ideas flow freely, and don't worry about perfection — this is your personal plan for transformation! Here's a template:

The Steps to My Dreams Are...

Family:

Finance:

Health:

Career:

Friends:

Love:

Leisure:

Growth:

Step 3: Identify Subtle Shifts

Look for small changes you can make in your daily habits to support your goals. This might mean dedicating more time to planning and working on your dreams instead of engaging in less productive activities. Consider how you spend your free time and find ways to use it more wisely to move closer to your dreams. To help you identify these subtle shifts, ask yourself the following questions — and take a few moments to write down your answers in your journal.

- Are there any activities I can reduce or eliminate to make more time for my goals?

  Consider cutting back on time spent watching TV, scrolling through social media, or other nonessential activities.

- What small changes can I make to my routine to support my goals?

  For example, waking up an hour earlier to work on your dreams, incorporating a daily walk for better health, or setting aside specific times for learning and development.

- How can I integrate goal-oriented tasks into my daily schedule?

Identify pockets of time that can be used more efficiently, such as listening to educational podcasts during your commute or using lunch breaks for reading relevant books.

- What habits can I develop to stay motivated and focused?

  Consider implementing daily affirmations, maintaining a journal to track progress, or setting weekly goals to keep yourself on track.

List three simple actions you plan to implement.

Step 4: Implement and Adjust

Start making these subtle shifts in your daily routine. Incorporate new habits gradually and be consistent. Keep track of your progress and adjust your actions as needed to stay aligned with your goals.

- **Weekly reflection:** At the end of each week, reflect on your progress. What worked well? What challenges did you face?
- **Adjust as needed:** Make adjustments to your habits if necessary. The goal is to find a sustainable routine that consistently brings you closer to your dream.

Step 5: Stay Motivated and Celebrate Small Wins

Remind yourself of your big dream regularly. Visualize your success and feel the excitement of achieving it. Use your Midlife Mantra to stay motivated and keep pushing forward, even when the going gets tough.

- **Recognize progress:** Celebrate your progress, no matter how small. Recognize that each little change brings you closer to your big dream.
- **Share your achievements:** Share your goals and progress

with a friend or accountability partner. Their support and encouragement can keep you motivated.

By following these steps and making intentional, subtle shifts in your daily habits, you'll be able to create the quantum leaps necessary to achieve your big dreams.

Coming Up

If you're concerned about making mistakes during the construction phase of your new life, the next chapter will put your mind at ease. Mistakes are invaluable opportunities to reset, regroup, and revise your goals, methods, and habits. In the upcoming chapter, you'll create a My Mistakes Roadmap, helping you find purpose and meaning in each misstep so you can view them not as regrets, but as stepping stones on your midlife journey. This transformative approach to viewing our mistakes is a game changer for healing, building confidence, and moving forward.

11

EMBRACE MISTAKES

You can't connect the dots looking forward; you can only connect them looking backwards. So, you have to trust that the dots will somehow connect in your future. You have to trust in something — your gut, destiny, life, karma, whatever. This approach has never let me down, and it has made all the difference in my life.

— Steve Jobs, Stanford University Commencement Address, June 12, 2005

I stood in the nearly empty living room of my apartment, surrounded by stacks of bins filled with camping supplies, my brand-new shiny red Coleman grill, and the remnants of my wardrobe — shorts, tank tops, and flip-flops. Not a single pair of sexy but uncomfortable high heels was in sight. The stark emptiness of the room mirrored the blank slate of my impending adventure. I picked up the latest iteration of my lengthy to-do list, scanning the tasks that needed to be completed before I could finally hit the road:

- ✓ Sell or donate furniture
- ✓ Declutter all my belongings
- ✓ Sell my car
- ✓ Create new website

- ✓ Do a photo shoot
- ✓ Buy podcast equipment
- ✓ Hire podcast editor
- ✓ Become top sales consultant of the year
- ✓ Pay off debt
- ✓ Save money for RV down payment
- ✓ Save one year of living expenses

There were only two unchecked items, but they were the biggest hurdles of them all:

- ❑ Buy a 2022 Thor Delano 24FB
- ❑ Resign from my job

The time to set off into the desert sun had finally almost come. Despite my excitement about this highly anticipated and meticulously planned dream, tears began streaming down my face. My mind was overwhelmed with panic-stricken thoughts. My heart was racing, and I could feel anxiety washing over me. This nauseating feeling reminded me of just two years ago, back in Virginia, when I was at my lowest point — bawling my eyes out, overwhelmed with debt, illness, and grief.

Now here I was in Illinois, crying again. But why? I had a successful job, my debt was paid off, my body and mind were healthy, I had a savings account for the first time in my life, and I was finally going to fulfill my dreams and pursue my passions. I should be in a state of joy, but instead I was paralyzed by fear.

Up to this point, I had spent countless hours in therapy, in meditation, reading self-help books, and mindfully choosing healthier thoughts, expecting to have moved beyond this internal turmoil. Apparently not. I may not have conquered all my fears, but I knew what to do with them: face them. As the caretaker of my mind, I knew I had to regain control and delve into the darkness.

I closed my eyes and sat alone with my fears, feeling as though I were in a deep, dark cave filled with a gang of angry monsters. These nasty gremlins began shouting: *You'll get lonely out there! You could fail as a podcaster and writer! You'll run out of money! This is really ridiculous! Oh my gosh, this will become another one of your big mistakes! Don't do it. Just stay here in the darkness with us.*

What a bunch of bullies. But the truth is, they were naming every what-if that had been silently eating away at me. One of my favorite quotes from Marianne Williamson popped into my mind: "Our deepest fear is not that we are inadequate. Our deepest fear is that we are powerful beyond measure. It is our light, not our darkness, that most frightens us. We ask ourselves, 'Who am I to be brilliant, gorgeous, talented, fabulous?' Actually, who are you not to be?"

Marianne Williamson and my obnoxious internal bullies made me realize I wasn't afraid of sitting in the dark, but rather, I was scared of stepping into the light of my dreams. Ironically, the dark cave had become my new comfort zone, and the monsters had become my new friends. As a child, I had mastered the skills of approval-seeking, codependency, and perfectionism to protect myself from my external world, and now I was using these same skills to protect myself from my internal world. I was basically gaslighting and manipulating myself into staying in the dark. Not only was I terrified to unleash Wendy into the wild world for fear of not being good enough, but I was also scared to make another mistake.

I called a dear friend of mine, Amy, who had "talked me off the ledge" quite a few times in the past few years, and shared my fears in moving forward with my dreams. She listened oh so patiently as I cried and rambled on about all my what-ifs.

"What if I don't succeed in my business? What if I don't like living in an RV? What if I get lonely? What if I'm making a big mistake?"

Amy said to me, "What if you succeed in your business? What if you love living in an RV? What if you enjoy your own company?

What if this becomes your greatest endeavor ever? What if you gave yourself permission to leap?"

My tears stopped flowing down my face as the positive flip side of my what-ifs began flowing through my mind.

Amy went on to say, "Wendy, everything has unfolded perfectly to bring you to this point. You're the one who's always telling me, 'Mistakes are simply opportunities for growth.'"

"Oh crap, did I say that? Yikes. I guess I'd better practice what I preach then!"

We both laughed, and then she said, "Besides, you're not stuck with anything. If you don't like it, you can pivot and do something else. Now go get that damn RV of yours!"

Instead of Amy "talking me off the ledge" like she had in the past, this time she "pushed me off the ledge" with her words of wisdom and encouragement. Her bold challenge was the catalyst I needed to break free from my fears and fully step into my light. It was the push that propelled me forward, giving me the courage to embark on my dreams with newfound determination and confidence.

Completing My To-Do List

Determined to get the Thor Delano 24FB motorhome I had dreamed about for two years, I managed to find the last one available in the entire country. On October 24, 2021, I flew from Chicago to Nashville, Tennessee, to meet my dazzling dream on wheels. As my taxi pulled into the Camping World dealership, I felt like I was being thrown into a vast sea of RVs. Rows and rows of motorhomes and trailers stretched out before me — some short, some tall, some big, some small. My eyes eagerly scanned the lot for my black beauty with blue and silver stripes, but she was nowhere to be found. *Where is she? Oh gosh, did they sell her? Noooo!*

Clutching my hot-off-the-press cashier's check and feeling a swarm of butterflies in my stomach, I walked into the sales office. A team of eager salesmen greeted me, ready to make their next big deal. Little did they know, they wouldn't need to sell me on anything — I was already sold.

Excited and nervous, I introduced myself, "Hi, I'm Wendy! I called yesterday about the 2022 Thor Delano 24FB, and I was told you have one left in stock. I just flew all the way from Chicago to buy it. Please tell me you didn't sell it."

With a warm Southern drawl, one of the gentlemen responded, "Howdy, ma'am. I'm Randy. I spoke to you yesterday. Don't you worry about a thang. I've got your new camper in the warehouse getting all spiffied up for ya'!"

Breathing a sigh of relief, I exclaimed, "Oh, thank God! Phew!" Then, as if requesting to see my newborn baby in the nursery, I asked, "Can I see her?"

"Not only can you see your new camper, but you can also take 'er on a test-drive!" Randy replied.

Test-drive? Eeek! I'd taken Honda Accords and scooters on test-drives, but never a twenty-five-foot-long, twelve-thousand-pound motorhome — or as they say in Tennessee, "camper." *Crap. Should I have taken an RV driving course or something? Oh no, how did I leave this important detail off my to-do list? I'm doomed.* My nerves kicked in, and I started to doubt my decision again.

Randy must've noticed the sweat beads forming on my forehead. Whether he was being a good salesman or a good person, he patted me on the back reassuringly, just like my dad would do, and said, "I'll teach you how to drive. You'll be great!"

We walked into the warehouse; a bustling hub filled with just-sold motorhomes. Mechanics were busy tightening bolts, and the cleaning crew polished shiny rims, preparing each vehicle for its new owners. Nestled among the towering forty-five-foot Class A motorhomes, there she was — my gorgeous, sparkling new life on wheels.

Like a child spotting her brand-new bicycle on Christmas morning, I dashed over with my arms flailing in excitement. I threw myself onto her freshly polished hood, hugging it tightly. "Ahhh," I sighed in pure bliss. Randy, beaming with amusement, approached and said, "Well, I've been doing this for over thirty years, and I ain't seen anyone more excited to buy a camper!"

With a warm smile, Randy opened the side door of the RV. The steps glided out from underneath the carriage like magic, and the bright interior lights flickered on, casting a welcoming glow. In his best Vanna White impression, Randy gracefully waved his arm toward the door, inviting me to step inside and explore my new home.

Grinning from ear to ear and with my eyes practically popping out of their sockets, I stepped into my new home on wheels and marveled at its beauty. I had spent two years obsessively watching videos, taking virtual tours, and studying every material and measurement, and she was everything I had dreamed of — and then some: the Murphy bed that effortlessly popped out of the wall with the push of a button, the plush beige leatherette cushions in the dinette that would soon become my podcast studio, and the compact kitchen equipped with a convection oven, two-burner propane stove, and stainless-steel fridge waiting to be filled with food for the road. Every detail was perfect. I felt an overwhelming sense of belonging — at home in my new house, my new life, and my new self.

"Well, what's her name gonna be?" Randy asked with a grin.

"Felisha, as in 'Bye Felisha' from the movie *Friday*," I replied, laughing.

Chuckling, Randy handed me the keys. After a nerve-wracking yet successful test-drive through the winding hills of Nashville, I returned to the dealership with a newfound sense of confidence. I handed over my hefty cashier's check, signed on the dotted line, and eagerly hopped into the captain's chair. The team of salesmen, now my enthusiastic cheerleaders, gathered outside, waving and shouting encouragement as I drove off the lot.

As I veered onto the highway for the eight-hour drive back to Chicago, I shouted aloud, "Felisha, we did it! We fucking did it! Yesssss!" With the window down, feeling the cool autumn breeze through my hair, I cranked up the radio and blasted Tom Cochrane's "Life Is a Highway." My dream was unfolding before my eyes, and I was loving every second of it.

Sitting in my captain's chair high above the highway, I waved at the cars zooming past, catching glimpses of their drivers doing double takes at the girl with the big hair driving the big RV. Some vehicles even slowed down to take a better look at Miss Felisha, admiring her luscious curves and sparkly stripes.

As I cruised through the Tennessee mountains, the vibrant orange and yellow leaves falling from the trees caught my eye, reminding me of the leaves painted on my brother's urn. I felt the warmth of his smile and could almost hear his voice from above: *Sis, I'm so proud of you. You got this.*

Tears began streaming down my face, but these tears were different from those of the past few years. These were tears of joy — the feeling for which I'd been yearning for so long. I thought to myself, *It's possible to find happiness again. Yes, bro, I got this.*

With that realization, I mentally checked off one of the last two items on my to-do list: Buy a 2022 Thor Delano 24FB. Done!

My Last Day

Exhausted yet exhilarated, I piloted Felisha into Chicago that night amid a cold, pouring rain. With all my furniture sold, I stayed with my friend Kae and her husband, Gary. I needed a good night's rest because tomorrow was the day I would cross off the last item on my list: Resign from my job.

On the morning of October 25, 2021, I walked into the sales model home where my manager, Jon, was working that day. I took a seat at the kitchen island while he finished a phone call. Although

I had been eagerly anticipating this moment for several months, I suddenly felt a wave of fear and uncertainty. Was I making the right decision?

The finality of the words I was about to say to Jon weighed heavily on me. My resignation meant returning to unemployment. Although the job wasn't fulfilling, it was still a job. This decision also signified the end of a pivotal chapter in my life — the chapter where I'd pushed through my misery and achieved significant goals. *You're doing so well, Wendy. You could always keep working here and live in the RV in Chicago*, I thought. I was grateful for Jon's prolonged phone call, which gave me extra time to contemplate my next critical life move.

The cascade of fearful thoughts was interrupted when I glanced at a painting of a butterfly above the fireplace. Butterflies had fascinated me since childhood. The painting took me back to fourth grade, when Miss Clark brought a mesh container into the classroom. Inside were leaves covered with tiny eggs. A few days later, I watched in amazement as the eggs hatched and caterpillars emerged. They immediately began eating their eggshells and munching on leaves to fatten up their little green bodies. Once plump, they found a safe spot along the container wall to spin a chrysalis.

Watching this wondrous transformation, little Wendy, with her pigtails and big green eyes, asked, "What is the caterpillar doing in there, Miss Clark?"

Miss Clark replied, "The caterpillar is growing legs, eyes, and wings to become a butterfly."

Growing more fascinated, I asked, "How will she come out of the chrysalis?"

"The butterfly will pump blood through its wings to gain enough strength to push through the chrysalis," Miss Clark explained.

Feeling sorry for the butterfly and eager to meet her, I handed my tiny red Crayola scissors to the teacher and said, "Miss Clark, let's cut the chrysalis and take out the butterfly!"

Miss Clark gently responded, "Oh no, Wendy, we can't do that. Without the struggle, the butterfly will lack the strength to fly and will die. The butterfly needs to struggle on her own to set herself free."

Snapping out of my fourth-grade flashback, I realized that over the past few years, I had undergone a similar metamorphosis. I had set the intentions of my dreams like the egg on the leaf, absorbed the nutrients and knowledge like the caterpillar, and transformed into a new woman like the butterfly inside the chrysalis. Resigning from my job was the struggle I needed to break through my comfy chrysalis and set myself free. The decision was made, and I was ready to fly.

Just then, I heard Jon's chipper and charming voice, "Heyyy! I'm surprised to see you here today! What brings you in?"

Of all the people I had worked for in the past thirty-five years, Jon was my favorite. Kind, generous, and compassionate, he was like a brother to me, providing the care and support I'd needed during this tumultuous chapter of my life. Jon and I always had a strong connection, as if he could read my mind, and he certainly did that morning too.

As I turned to look at him, my eyes filled with tears. His big smile quickly turned into a frown, and he gave a slight nod as if to say, *I know why you're here.*

My well-rehearsed resignation speech went out the window as I blurted out, "I bought an RV yesterday, so I'm taking off across the country to start my own show and become a writer."

I was nervous that my words might have upset Jon and ruined our friendship. But, as a true friend would, Jon responded with three beautiful words that still resonate loudly in my heart to this day: "Go be Wendy."

Those were the words I needed to hear as I gave that final push through my chrysalis. Tears flowing like a river, I gave Jon a big hug of pure gratitude, walked out the door, and checked off that final item on my to-do list.

Nudge, Nudge

Just as Amy gave me the nudge to buy the RV and Jon encouraged me to go be myself, I am here to offer you that same gentle push of encouragement. After all, that's what friends are for, right?

In this next section, you will create a My Mistakes Roadmap, a tool to help you find purpose and meaning in each misstep. This exercise will allow you to see your mistakes not as regrets, but as valuable stepping stones on your midlife journey, guiding you toward growth and self-discovery.

Creating your My Mistakes Roadmap is like charting the course of your metamorphosis. Just as the challenge inside the chrysalis transforms the butterfly, your mistakes ultimately give you the strength to emerge as a more resilient and empowered version of yourself. Embrace each misstep as an essential part of your journey, and use this roadmap to illuminate the lessons you've learned and the progress you've made.

By reframing your mistakes and viewing them as opportunities for growth, you'll find the courage to spread your wings and soar toward your dreams. So let's dive in.

My Mistakes Roadmap

Step 1: List Your Mistakes

Start by listing some significant mistakes or missteps you've made in the different categories of your life. Consider the following examples:

- **Family:** conflicts, misunderstandings, missed opportunities for connection
- **Finance:** poor investments, debt accumulation, overspending
- **Health:** neglecting your well-being, unhealthy habits, emotional eating

- **Career:** misguided job choices, staying in an unfulfilling job too long, putting up with an abusive boss
- **Friends:** lost friendships, failing to prioritize quality time with girlfriends
- **Love:** relationship issues, breakups, lack of self-love
- **Leisure:** trips you didn't take, hobbies you didn't pursue, focusing on work or family at the expense of free time
- **Growth:** not pursuing personal development, avoiding challenges

Step 2: Pick Your Most Pivotal Mistakes

From your list, choose the top four mistakes that had the most significant impact on your life. These are the pivotal missteps that shaped your journey. Write them down below or in your journal.

Mistake 1:
Mistake 2:
Mistake 3:
Mistake 4:

Step 3: Create Your Roadmap

To complete your My Mistakes Roadmap, reflect on the lessons you've learned from each mistake and how they've contributed to your growth, then outline a positive action you will take to counteract this mistake. Write out your answers to the following prompts in your journal or the *Women Waking Up Playbook* available at WomenWakingUp.com.

Because of this mistake, I now know... [Insert the lesson you learned.]

This mistake has helped me to... [Describe how the mistake has contributed to your growth.]

Moving forward, I will... [State a positive action you will take based on the lesson.]

By reframing your past mistakes, you'll transform them into valuable learning experiences that guide your journey forward. This exercise will serve as a powerful reminder of your resilience, your growth, and the wisdom you've gained.

Step 4: Embrace Your Journey

Finally, take a moment to appreciate your journey. Acknowledge that your mistakes have shaped you into the person you are today and equipped you with the knowledge and resilience to navigate the future. Embrace your past, present, and future with gratitude and self-compassion.

Remember, life isn't about mistakes; it's about opportunities for growth and learning. By transforming your perspective on past missteps, you empower yourself to move forward with confidence, wisdom, and a renewed sense of purpose. Your My Mistakes Roadmap is a testament to your strength and resilience, guiding you toward a brighter, more fulfilling future.

Coming Up

Congratulations on completing step 4, "Embrace and Explore." This step has been about dropping perfectionism, making mistakes, and simplifying the process of reinventing yourself one step at a time. To further solidify your progress, I encourage you to listen to the Embrace and Explore meditation in the FREEDOM Meditation Series. It's specifically designed to help you internalize the lessons you've learned and empower you to continue on your path with renewed vigor.

As we move forward, it's time to shift our focus to the present moment. Step 5, "Detach from Tomorrow," is all about letting go of rigid plans and embracing the beauty of spontaneity, miracles, and fun. While it's important to create your dreams and set your intentions, it's equally crucial to allow life to unfold naturally.

In chapter 12, we will explore the concept of the no-plan plan. We have been conditioned to plan out every aspect of our lives — education, career, family, and even daily routines. However, an overabundance of plans can stifle spontaneity, creativity, and joy. The second half of life offers a unique opportunity to let go, embrace the unknown, and go with the flow.

Let's embark on this next step with an open heart and a spirit of adventure. Say yes to the possibilities that come with living in the present moment, and get ready to follow the no-plan plan and have fun!

STEP

DETACH FROM TOMORROW

12

FOLLOW THE NO-PLAN PLAN AND HAVE FUN

Leap, and the net will appear.
— attributed to John Burroughs

With my to-do list completely checked off, there was nothing else left to do but get Felisha ready for the road. Over the next few days, the RV sat in the parking lot of Kae and Gary's condo as I transferred all my belongings from the stack of bins to the drawers of the RV, and, of course, stored my shiny red Coleman grill in Felisha's underbelly. With winter right around the corner, I had to move quickly to avoid any freezing of the water and sewer lines in the RV — a precaution I had learned about in my handy-dandy RV books.

Despite my diligent efforts to declutter over the past few months, squeezing everything into what felt like the size of a shoebox was still a daunting task — Felisha was too cluttered and bursting at the seams. As if playing a game of Tetris, I turned stuff upside down and inside out, trying to make it fit. Errr! Determined and frustrated, I pulled everything back out of the cabinets and drawers, laid it all over the floor of the RV, sat in the middle of it, and cried.

At that moment, the door opened, and in walked Kae. With

her hands on her hips, she looked down at me amid the pile of pots, pans, pillows, and pajamas and said, "Girrrrrl, what in the world are you doing?"

"I'm so annoyed! I can't get all this crap to fit! The forecast calls for freezing temperatures tomorrow night, and I need to get out of here! I don't even know where I'm going to drive this thing!"

Moving a stack of shirts to the side, Kae sat down on the floor across from me and looked me in the eye. Knowing that my tears had nothing to do with the clutter inside the RV and everything to do with the clutter of thoughts in my head, she said, "Take a deep breath. It's all going to be okay. Wendy, you've done such a great job over the past year of dreaming, planning, and checking off your to-do list. Now you just need to drop the plans and follow your heart. Have faith in yourself."

Kae always knew the right words to say just when I needed to hear them.

She continued, "Let me help you pare down some more and take some stuff to Goodwill. Do you really need all these cake pans?"

Wiping the tears from my face, I replied, "Well, what if I want to bake a cake or something?"

With a puzzled look, she said, "Wendy, you're not gonna be baking cakes in an RV park!"

We both giggled as I tossed the cake pans into the Goodwill pile. Kae and I whittled away at the pile on the floor, making decisions about what was truly necessary for my new RV life. Together, we managed to fit everything into the cabinets (including one six-inch cake pan...just in case).

As we worked, Kae's words resonated deeply with me. I realized this journey wasn't just about making everything fit perfectly in the RV; it was about embracing a new way of living and trusting myself to navigate whatever came my way. Grabbing the stack of USA road trip books that I had studied, highlighted, and dog-eared over the past year, I shoved them into the back of the closet, never to be looked at again. With my destination still unknown, it didn't even matter anymore because, in my eyes, I had already arrived exactly where I needed to be — my true self. I felt more ready than ever to hit the road and embark on my adventure.

Turning off the lights and locking the doors, I patted Felisha on the hood and said, "Sleep tight, Felisha. We have a long drive in the morning."

Pedal to the Metal

Waking up on November 5, 2021, I peeked out the window at Felisha in the parking lot and noticed a layer of frost on her hood — a clear sign it was time to hit the road. Kae and I sat at her kitchen table, savoring a cup of coffee together before saying our goodbyes.

"Are you ready?" Kae asked.

With excitement and a tinge of nervousness, I responded, "Ready as I'll ever be!"

"Did you decide where to go?" she inquired.

"Nope, I'm on the no-plan plan! I'll just follow the sun!" I replied with a grin.

Kae's voice quivered as she poured the rest of her coffee down the kitchen sink. "Well, I hate to run, but I hate goodbyes." We hugged each other tightly, both holding back tears, before Kae headed off to work.

Unlocking the driver's side door of the RV, I placed my foot onto the cab step of the chassis like I was a badass trucker, grabbed the steering wheel, and pulled myself up to plop my butt into the captain's chair. I started the engine, cranked up the heat, and did my final walk-through.

Cabinets closed — check!
Slide-out in — check!
Lights off — check!
Leveling jacks up — check!

Exterior doors locked — check!

Bike secure — check!

Sewer closed — check!

I locked the cabin door, hopped back into the captain's chair, and said aloud to myself, "Okay, I think we're ready! Wait, did I check the leveling jacks?" I hopped out of my chair again, unlocked the cabin door, stepped outside, and crouched down to look underneath the RV to make sure the leveling jacks were retracted.

Leveling jacks up — check!

I stepped back into the now warm-and-toasty Felisha, locked the door, hopped back into the captain's chair, and said, "Okay, *nowww* we're ready!"

"Oh wait, one more thing!" I reached down into my purse, grabbed a two-inch Wonder Woman plastic doll, and placed it on the dashboard so it faced out over the hood.

My little Wonder Woman served as a reminder of courage and strength during my entire RV journey, and she now hangs above my laptop while I write this book.

Cranking up the speakers to what soon became my "takeoff" song, I played Willie Nelson's classic "On the Road Again" and pulled out of the parking lot and onto the road. As I watched the city of Chicago fade in my rearview mirror, a mix of emotions washed over me. This was it — the moment I had been dreaming of and planning for. It was time to step fully into my new life, with no plans, just a direction: toward the sun and whatever adventures lay ahead.

My First Stop

Given that winter had begun and I was in the heart of the Midwest, my route options were limited. Wisconsin, Iowa, Indiana, and Kentucky were already experiencing freezing temperatures, which wouldn't be good for Felisha's new pipes or for me, a novice RVer, to deal with.

Cruising south down Interstate 55, I glanced at the navigation screen, checked my weather app, and concluded that my best option was to head to St. Louis, Missouri, for my first night. Embracing the spontaneity and serendipity of my new no-plan plan, I couldn't help but smile at the coincidence: St. Louis was my birthplace, a city I hadn't visited in forty years. With my brother's orange and yellow decorated urn by my side, it felt fitting to pay a visit to the house where we grew up. It was as if the universe was guiding me back to my roots as the starting point of this grand adventure.

Leaving the quiet cornfields of Illinois and pulling into the bustling city of St. Louis, I was flooded with memories. I recalled performing at a dance recital on one of the famous Gateway Arch riverboats when I was just six years old. The sun beamed brightly over the Mississippi River, blinding me as I navigated away from the city center.

Without an address and relying solely on childhood memories, I drove toward my old neighborhood. As I spotted the familiar 84 Lumber Company on the side of the highway — the place where I used to tag along with my dad on weekends to gather wood for his next house project — I knew I was close. I took the next exit, feeling a rush of nostalgia.

"This has got to be it," I murmured to myself as I ventured deeper into the area that once was home.

With the steep hills in my old neighborhood and my beginner driving skills, I thought it best to park the RV at the bottom and walk to my childhood home. I pulled into the parking lot of a hardware store that I didn't recognize, but then realized it was once the field where my brother and I played baseball. I laughed aloud, imagining Bryan and me racing to the concessions stand to buy Coca-Cola and Big League Chew bubble gum.

"Last one there's a rotten egg!" he would shout as his long legs sprinted past me.

I unlocked the exterior door to the cabinet filled with camping supplies, grabbed my hiking backpack, tossed a jug of water and my brother's urn in the bag, and set out to find my old house. As I took a stroll down memory lane, I passed by my bus stop and the remnants of the fort I built with my buddy James. I walked up the steep hill where I had my Big Wheel accident, and there, at the very end of the street, was my red brick house, just as I remembered it.

Considering this was a very rural area, residents peeked out their windows, curious about the woman wandering around their neighborhood. I walked up onto the front porch of my old house and knocked on the door. A little boy answered.

Feeling like a kid again, as if I were going to ask him to come out and play, I said, "Hi! I'm Wendy!"

Clearly surprised to have a visitor, he replied, "Hi. I'll get my dad."

As I waited for his dad, I noticed a little girl in the front window of what used to be my bedroom, playing with her dolls. I smiled, thinking of little Wendy teaching school to her stuffed animals.

A man came to the door. "Hello there," he greeted me.

"Hi. I'm Wendy! My parents built this house about forty years ago. I haven't been back here since I was nine years old, and I just wanted to see it again."

"Oh wow, welcome back! Does it still look the same?" the man asked.

"It actually does," I replied. "Lots of good memories of my brother and me growing up here."

He smiled. "What a coincidence. I have one daughter and son too."

"Do they like the tire swing on the big oak tree that my dad hung up for us?" I asked.

"Well, they did, but unfortunately, that old oak tree died a couple of years ago," he responded sadly.

"That's a coincidence too. My brother died a couple of years ago."

"I'm so sorry," he said.

"Thank you," I said. "I won't keep you much longer. Do you mind if I walk around a bit?"

"Of course, take your time," the man kindly said.

I walked to the side of the house and sat on the stump of the old oak tree. I glanced down at the ground and noticed two acorns joined together by the tips of their wooden "hats," as my brother and I used to call them. I reached into my backpack, pulled out the urn, and sprinkled a pinch of Bryan's ashes onto the acorn siblings. Expecting to be overwhelmed with feelings of sadness, I surprisingly felt very much at peace, at home in more ways than one.

I made the hike back down the hill and drove to a nearby campground for the night. Not only would it be my first time hooking up the RV on my own, but it would also be my first night sleeping in the RV — just me, myself, and I.

First Night in the RV

With my long, thick, wavy hair styled to perfection, bright pink lipstick on, and dressed in Lululemon pants, I probably didn't fit the typical camper persona. The lady at the front desk certainly thought so. She gave me a once-over, her eyes lingering on my polished look, and said, "Well, it looks like you'll need some help backing up your camper and hooking up the water and sewer lines, darlin'."

Her assumption irked me, and my newfound courage, which had quadrupled over the past few weeks, surged. Feeling like the Wonder Woman standing proudly on my dashboard, I shot her a confident smile and replied, "Nope, I got this."

Despite the temptation to check my manuals for a refresher, I decided to trust my instincts and go for it. With an audience of seasoned campers watching intently, I backed Felisha into her RV site like a pro, extended the slide-out, dropped the leveling jacks, plugged in the electric cord, hooked up the water line, attached the sewer hose, and finally, settled into my comfy new camping chair by the campfire with a big glass of wine.

Closing my eyes, feeling the warmth of the fire on my feet, and smelling the fresh burning wood, I thought to myself, *The no-plan plan sure is exciting. I wonder where I'll go tomorrow.*

Drop Your Plans

We have been taught to plan out everything in our lives — plans for education, building a career, raising kids, and even minute-to-minute plans for every day of the week. So. Many. Plans. While planning can bring structure and a sense of control, it often leaves no room for spontaneity, miracles, and fun. It's easy to become so wrapped up in our plans that we forget to enjoy the journey itself.

Though it's important to create your dreams and set your intentions, it's imperative to then allow life to unfold. The second half of life is a great opportunity to let go a little (or a lot), embrace the unknown, and go with the flow. This chapter is about discovering the joy and freedom that come from releasing rigid plans and embracing a more spontaneous approach to life.

The Beauty of Spontaneity

Spontaneity invites us to step outside our comfort zone and experience life in unexpected and delightful ways. It's about saying yes to opportunities that come our way, even if they weren't part of the plan. When we allow ourselves to be spontaneous, we open the door to new experiences, new people, and new perspectives that enrich our lives in ways we never could have predicted.

Imagine waking up one day with no set agenda. Instead of following your usual routine, you decide to explore a new part of town, try a new hobby, or simply take a leisurely walk in nature. These unplanned moments can bring a sense of adventure and joy that rigid plans often can't provide.

Embracing the Unknown

Letting go of detailed plans doesn't mean abandoning your dreams or goals. It's about trusting the process and having faith that things will unfold as they should. Life is full of surprises, and sometimes the best experiences come from the unexpected twists and turns.

Consider the possibility that not having everything mapped out can lead to wonderful discoveries. By being open to the unknown, you allow room for miracles and serendipity. You might meet someone who changes your life, stumble upon a new passion, or find yourself in a situation that brings profound happiness.

Living in the Present Moment

One of the greatest benefits of the no-plan plan is that it encourages us to live in the present moment. When we're not constantly focused on what's next, we can fully appreciate what's happening right now. This mindfulness can lead to deeper connections with ourselves and others, greater gratitude, and a more fulfilling life.

Discovering New Hobbies and Interests

When we let go of rigid plans, we create space to discover new hobbies and interests. You might find a new passion for painting, dancing, gardening, or cooking. These activities not only bring joy but also help you connect with yourself on a deeper level.

Building New Connections

Being open to spontaneity also means being open to new people. You never know when a chance encounter might lead to a meaningful friendship or even a romantic relationship. By stepping out of your comfort zone, you increase the chances of meeting people who can enrich your life.

Creating New Energy

Living a more spontaneous life infuses your days with confidence. The excitement of not knowing exactly what's going to happen next keeps life interesting and fun. This new energy can boost your creativity, improve your mood, and make you feel more alive.

Ways to Embrace the No-Plan Plan

- **Break your routine:** Start small by breaking your daily routine. Take a different route to work, try a new coffee shop, or switch up your exercise routine. These little changes can make your day feel fresh and exciting.
- **Say yes more often:** Challenge yourself to say yes to invitations and opportunities that you might usually decline. Whether it's a spontaneous road trip, a last-minute dinner with friends, or trying a new activity, saying yes can lead to memorable experiences.
- **Practice mindfulness:** Focus on being present in each moment. Pay attention to your surroundings, engage fully in conversations, and savor your meals. Mindfulness helps you appreciate the here and now.
- **Leave gaps in your schedule:** Instead of filling every hour with tasks, leave some gaps in your schedule for unplanned activities. Use this time to relax, explore, or simply do nothing.
- **Trust your intuition:** Allow your intuition to guide you. If something feels right, go for it, even if it wasn't part of the plan. Trusting yourself can lead to amazing opportunities.

As we embrace the no-plan plan, we find that life becomes more vibrant and fulfilling. Letting go of rigid plans allows us to experience the beauty of spontaneity, the joy of new discoveries, and the thrill of living in the present moment. By being open to the unknown, we create a life filled with adventure, creativity, and unexpected pleasures.

Next, you will learn the Spontaneity Spark method, designed to help you break free from routine, embrace the unknown, and discover new passions and joys. By integrating this method into your life, you'll build new energy and excitement, enriching your midlife journey with unexpected pleasures and meaningful experiences. Get ready to embrace the unknown and have fun along the way!

The Spontaneity Spark Method

Step 1: Create a Spontaneity Jar

Materials: A jar, slips of paper, and a pen.

Instructions: Write down various spontaneous activities or challenges on the slips of paper — aim for at least ten to twenty to get started. See below for a list of examples, or come up with your own. Fold each slip, and place them in the jar.

Examples of activities:

Take a dance class
Visit a local museum
Try a new restaurant
Take a different route to work
Spend a day hiking in a nearby park
Attend a community event or festival
Visit a pet shop
Cook a new recipe
Start a conversation with a stranger
Volunteer for a cause you're passionate about
Write a poem or paint a picture
Try a new cuisine
Visit a new place
Go on a mini road trip
Join a meetup group
Have a tech-free day
Try a new exercise
Perform a random act of kindness
Host a potluck
Go stargazing
Write a letter
Attend a social event
Plant a garden
Try a new hobby
Read a book in a genre you don't usually read
Visit a farmers market

Step 2: Draw an Activity Weekly

Instructions: Set a specific day, and draw an activity from the Spontaneity Jar on that day each week. This will add an element of excitement and anticipation to your week.

Commitment: Whatever activity you draw, commit to doing it within the next week. This will help you stay accountable and ensure you're consistently stepping out of your comfort zone.

Step 3: Reflect and Record

Journal prompt: After completing each spontaneous activity, take a few moments to reflect on the experience. Write down your thoughts in a journal. What did you enjoy? What did you learn? How did it make you feel?

Growth tracking: Over time, look back at your journal entries to see how these experiences have contributed to your personal growth, happiness, and sense of adventure.

Step 4: Share Your Experiences

Social circle: Share your spontaneous adventures with friends or family — whether by telling them about your experiences or inviting them to join you. You might just inspire them to create their own Spontaneity Jar too!

Step 5: Use a Spontaneity Calendar

Visual representation: Create a calendar where you can mark the dates of your spontaneous activities. This will serve as a visual reminder of your commitment to living a more spontaneous and adventurous life.

Highlighting favorites: Use stickers or colors to highlight the activities you enjoyed the most. This will help you identify your new favorite hobbies, places, and experiences.

Step 6: Celebrate Small Wins

Acknowledgment: Celebrate each completed activity, no matter how big or small. Recognize the courage it took to step out of your comfort zone.

Rewarding Yourself: Treat yourself to something special after completing a certain number of activities. For example, after every five activities, reward yourself with a small gift or treat.

By embracing the no-plan plan and implementing the Spontaneity Spark method, you've taken a significant step toward infusing your life with more joy, adventure, and creativity. Allowing yourself to break free from rigid plans and explore new experiences not only enriches your daily life but also opens doors to unexpected opportunities and personal growth. Remember, life is a journey meant to be enjoyed, and sometimes the most memorable moments come from the unplanned and the spontaneous.

As you continue on your journey of midlife reinvention, remember that embracing spontaneity and living in the present moment can lead to unexpected treasures. Keep your Spontaneity Jar close and let it guide you to new adventures, hobbies, and connections. The freedom and fulfillment you seek are often just a spontaneous decision away.

Coming Up

In the next chapter, you'll learn the Trigger to Treasure technique, a powerful method to transform moments of frustration and angst into opportunities for growth and acceptance. Through positive affirmation, acceptance of what cannot be changed, taking responsibility for what can be changed, and disconnecting from the triggering situation with meditation and other methods, you'll discover the path to achieving freedom within yourself and your life. Get ready to release control and get free!

13

RELEASE CONTROL TO GET FREE

There's nothing negative about being triggered. It's a calling to heal our wounds.

— Dr. Nicole LePera

After I spent that first magical night in St. Louis, I embarked on a journey southward, chasing the warmth of the sun. My adventure led me to visit my Aunt Annie in Arkansas, where we laughed and chatted over a pitcher of margaritas. In Oklahoma, I explored the whimsical Totem Pole Park, capturing the charm of its hand-carved structures on camera to share with my Instagram fans. At Cadillac Ranch in Texas, I added my mark to the quirky artistry, spray-painting "Wendy was here!" in fluorescent pink. Continuing my trek along the iconic Route 66, I finally arrived in the enchanting city of Santa Fe, New Mexico.

By this point, I had become adept at maneuvering the RV through bustling traffic, seamlessly navigating the highways and byways. I had also mastered the art of setting up the RV at various campgrounds, efficiently hooking up the utilities upon arrival and unhooking them when it was time to depart. With each new stop, my confidence grew and I felt more at home in my new life on the road.

With the long drive from Illinois to New Mexico beginning to take its toll, I realized that the no-plan plan was nudging me toward one clear priority: rest and relaxation. It dawned on me that there was no need to rush to the next destination as if I had some kind of deadline or end point in sight. *Vacation!* The word rolled around in my mind, and I liked how it sounded. It felt like I was on a permanent vacation, with no urgency to move on. So instead of staying at the Santa Fe KOA for just a night or two, as I had at other campgrounds, I decided to book an entire week.

My campsite was nestled among towering pine trees, providing the perfect spot to hang up my brand-new hammock. The shiny blue nylon hammock had been squished inside one of those plastic storage bins back in Chicago, and now it could finally stretch out and breathe in the open air. With a glass of wine in hand, I eagerly plopped down into the hammock, which immediately swung back and nearly sent me tumbling onto the ground. Laughing to myself, I thought about how hilarious it would've been if I had ended up sprawled out in the dirt.

Careful not to spill my wine, I fished my phone out of my pocket to capture the peaceful scene before me for my Instagram story. The RV gleamed in the bright New Mexico sunlight, my trusty red Coleman grill stood ready to cook up the piece of fresh salmon I'd just bought, and my two comfy gray camping chairs waited patiently beneath the silver-and-blue-striped awning. I typed out the caption "Scene from Santa Fe" with a smiley face emoji, and hit *Post*.

As I reclined back into my hammock, feeling it wrap around me like a snug chrysalis, I could sense the warmth of the desert sun on my face and the crisp mountain air filling my lungs. *Ahhh, this is heaven*, I thought, as I closed my eyes and let the serenity of the moment wash over me.

Suddenly, I heard the familiar ding of my phone and saw an Instagram notification pop up on my screen. Over the past couple of weeks, my phone had been buzzing nonstop with messages from people all around the world, curious about my RV adventures and eager to share their own dreams of hitting the open road.

"I've always wanted to take an RV trip along the Pacific Coast Highway!"

"How did you learn to drive an RV? You are so brave!"

"I love what you're doing! I can't wait to see where you go next!"

Most of the comments were filled with positivity and excitement, fueling my enthusiasm for this new chapter in my life. However, every so often, a nasty comment would sneak in — a harsh reminder of what the social media world calls trolls.

"You make me cringe."

"All that sitting is making you fat. Drive that RV to a gym."

"You're a spoiled brat. Did your rich boyfriend buy you that fancy RV?"

I had learned to treat these trolls just like I had dealt with the negative thoughts that used to plague my mind: with my trusty Stop, Drop, and Roll method. I stopped the trolls by blocking them from my page, dropped their nasty comments by deleting them from my post, and rolled on by replacing their negativity with something positive.

"You make me smile!"

"All that sitting is making you happy in your own skin. Drive that RV to a spa!"

"You're amazing! I'm so proud of you for buying a fancy RV all by yourself!"

But one particular troll hit a nerve when I read this message on my screen:

"Why did you bother buying two chairs when it's just you? Trying to pretend you're not lonely? Face it — nobody wants an old, divorced woman!"

That comment cut deeper than the others. This troll's comment wasn't just a casual jab — it struck at the core of the insecurities I thought I had left behind. I tried to apply my usual Stop, Drop, and

Roll method, but I found myself stuck at the Roll part, unable to muster any positive thoughts about myself. My mind spiraled into a storm of negativity.

I gently placed my glass of wine on the ground, curled up tightly in the hammock until only a sliver of light peeked through, and let the tears roll down my cheeks. I was angry that some stranger on the internet had the power to hijack my peaceful moment, but even more so, I was furious with myself for letting it happen. *I should be stronger than this. Why am I letting this troll's words get to me?*

Kristina to the Rescue

I realized that, just as my deep-rooted issues had followed me from Virginia to Illinois, they had also accompanied me to New Mexico. But fortunately, so had the voice of my therapist, Kristina. Amid the chaotic thoughts swirling in my mind, I could hear Kristina's calm and familiar question, the one she often asked me during our sessions: *Where are you feeling this hurt?*

Almost as if I were back in her Chicago office, I responded silently, *In my heart.*

Close your eyes, take a deep breath, and allow the feelings to surface, Kristina's voice echoed in my mind.

More tears flowed as I followed her gentle guidance.

What are you feeling? Kristina's voice inquired.

I'm angry that he said that to me. What a jerk! I screamed in my head.

As Kristina would usually do, she pushed me to dig deeper: *What specifically about his comments made you angry?*

It's the fact that he called me a lonely old divorced woman, I admitted.

Kristina had a unique way of helping me see the truth beneath my fears by flipping the problem on its head. *Is there any truth to what he said?*

Trying to be completely honest with Kristina, or myself really, I reluctantly replied, *Well, maybe. I am a divorced woman, and I'm turning fifty next week. Even though this new adventure is exciting right now, I'm scared that once the novelty wears off, I'll feel lonely. I'm afraid I'll wish I had someone sitting in that empty gray chair next to me, sharing a glass of wine by the campfire.*

As soon as I acknowledged those feelings, I knew the word *afraid* was like a flashing neon sign for the next question in my internal therapy session: *Why are you afraid to wish for a loving partner in life?*

Without missing a beat, I answered, *I'm afraid I'm not worthy of a loving partner, but mostly I'm afraid of...* I hesitated, the words sticking in my throat.

Mostly you're afraid of what? the voice in my head gently urged me to continue.

With my eyes tightly shut, I felt the hammock swaying in the breeze, my heart pounding in my chest. I desperately wanted to conclude this impromptu therapy session so I could return to the peace I had felt just moments ago. But I knew that to truly move forward, I had to face the truth that lay buried beneath my pain.

I'm mostly afraid of being abandoned, I finally admitted, the words coming out in a whisper, as if saying them aloud might make them too real.

There it was, that old, familiar fear of abandonment rearing its ugly head once again. No matter how much work I had done, how far I had come, this deep-seated issue still lingered, waiting for moments like this to remind me it hadn't completely left.

Despite making significant progress in my Wheel of Midlife, there was one area that remained a real struggle for me — love. I had done the work: journaling, reflecting, setting goals, even taking small steps toward opening my heart. But when it came to matters of the heart, I had built walls so high that even I couldn't see over them. While the other areas of my life had steadily improved, love was the one piece of the puzzle I couldn't quite figure out.

My past was marked by a series of intense, passionate relationships that had each ended in pain and heartache. Twice married and twice divorced, I had loved deeply, but those loves had left scars, making me fearful of opening myself up to love again. The wounds from those experiences ran deep, and the thought of another attempt at love felt overwhelming. My heart had been shattered too many times, and I wasn't sure it could survive another break.

So I had sidestepped love, focusing on everything else — career, health, personal growth — anything that felt safer, more controllable. But now, sitting in that hammock, I couldn't escape the realization that by avoiding love, I was also avoiding a crucial part of my own happiness. And yet the fear of falling in love again, of risking that kind of vulnerability, was paralyzing. My heart, once so eager to give and receive love, had become guarded, hesitant to even entertain the possibility of another romantic connection.

Despite the sting of that troll's comment, I wasn't about to let it derail my journey. Yes, it had struck a nerve, dredging up old wounds, but I had come too far to let fear, especially the fear of abandonment, dictate my future. I was on a mission to uncover the treasure hidden beneath the trauma, and I was determined not to let this moment of doubt undo all the progress I had made.

That quiet moment, nestled in my hammock, felt like déjà vu — a scene replaying from the dark night of my soul a year ago. Once again, I found myself face-to-face with little Wendy, the younger version of myself who had long carried the burden of these fears. I took a deep breath, feeling the weight of the moment and the significance of what I was about to say.

Out loud, I spoke with a firm but gentle resolve, "Today, we are taking off the heavy armor guarding your heart. We are making space for love to come in, and we will welcome it with open arms."

The words hung in the air, a promise to little Wendy and to

myself that I would no longer let past hurts keep me from the love and connection I deserved. It was time to let go of the armor that had once protected me but now only served to keep love out.

Manifesting New Love

As if drawing back the curtains to let in the morning light, I reached up and peeled away the fabric of the hammock, welcoming the warmth of the sunshine back into my space. With a few scooches and twists, I maneuvered myself out of the hammock and back onto solid ground. I picked up my glass of wine from where it rested in the dirt and placed it gently on a small plastic table nestled between the two gray chairs. The sun's rays sparkled on the rim of the glass, and I could feel the shift within me — an invitation to open up, to explore, and to heal.

I stepped into the RV and reached for my new Wonder Woman journal and a pen. I settled into one of the gray chairs, feeling the sturdy comfort beneath me, and opened the journal to its very first page. With a deep breath, I began to write — not about the superficial Mr. Right I had once envisioned, with his perfect height, weight, and bank account, but about the kind of relationship I truly desired in this new chapter of my life.

This time, my focus wasn't on the man himself but on the connection we would share. I envisioned a partner who loved Wendy for Wendy — a man who would encourage me to be unapologetically myself and support me in shining my light brightly onto the world. Gone were the days of seeking approval from others; now I was searching for someone who adored me as much as I had learned to adore myself.

I realized that with this newfound love and respect for who I am, I no longer needed a man to complete me. My life was already sweet enough, and the partner I sought would be the sprinkles on top — adding color and joy but never overshadowing the cake itself.

With this perspective, I wrote freely, letting my thoughts and desires flow onto the pages for over an hour. I crafted the vision of a beautiful, loving, and caring relationship, believing that if I could manifest everything else in my life, I could certainly create this too.

Finally, I returned to the Stop, Drop, and Roll method, determined to rewrite the narrative that the troll's comment had tried to inscribe in my mind. I penned the words with intention and affirmation:

I am a strong, vibrant woman who is open to giving and receiving love.

As I closed the journal, a sense of peace washed over me. I was no longer angry at the troll who had triggered my trauma. Instead, I felt a deep gratitude for the shift in my consciousness that had come from facing this challenge head-on. What initially felt like an attack had turned into an opportunity for growth — a boost to my well-being and a reaffirmation of my journey. In that moment, I realized that every trigger, every obstacle, every nudge, was guiding me closer to the woman I was meant to be.

Understanding Triggers

So what exactly are triggers? Triggers are people, places, things, or situations that evoke an emotional response, often rooted in past experiences or traumas. When you encounter something that reminds your brain and body of a previous traumatic event, your system may react by entering fight-or-flight mode as a way of protecting you from perceived harm. These reminders can come in many forms — such as a specific smell, sight, or sound — but more often than not, they show up as words or actions from someone else. A single comment, like the one I received from that troll online, can strike a nerve and instantly transport you back to a moment of shame, fear, or pain.

For instance, imagine that a loved one passed away a few years ago on Christmas Day. Now every year when you hear Christmas songs playing in the grocery store, your brain associates those melodies with your loss, and suddenly you find yourself tearing up in the middle of the aisle. That's a trigger — your body's way of connecting the present moment with an emotional event from your past.

Or perhaps as a child, you were often criticized by your father, who told you that you couldn't do anything right. Now as an adult, whenever your boss walks into your office to discuss your latest project, you might feel an overwhelming sense of anxiety or even anger if he points out something he doesn't like. That reaction stems from a trigger — a connection between your boss's critique and the harsh words you heard as a child.

Triggers can also arise from past experiences that echo into the present — even if we don't immediately see the link. Take, for example, the time in high school when you were giving a book report in English class and the teacher embarrassed you in front of everyone. Years later, being asked to speak in front of a group might stir up that same old wave of embarrassment or dread. In fact, this last example is a true story from my life. It happened to me in eleventh grade, and that moment stayed with me for years. But here's the empowering part: I transformed that trigger into a treasure by becoming a motivational speaker. Take that, Miss Murphy!

Triggers can be powerful, but they also present an opportunity. When you recognize them, you can work to transform them from sources of pain into sources of strength. By understanding your triggers, you can begin to reclaim your power, allowing these moments to propel you forward rather than hold you back.

Reacting to Triggers

Everyone reacts to triggers in their own unique way. For some, triggers can lead to panic, tears, outbursts, or withdrawal from others.

It's as if the person is reliving that past traumatic experience in the present moment. Whether it's a minor trauma — a "little *t*" — or a significant trauma — a "BIG *T*" — your brain and body can react as though the event is happening all over again. This reaction is quite similar to what happens in cases of PTS (post-traumatic stress), and it can come with a range of physical symptoms. When you're triggered, you might feel your heart start racing, break out in a cold sweat, experience vivid flashbacks of the event, or even suffer a full-blown panic attack. Trust me, I've been there, done that.

Sometimes, the effects of a trigger aren't immediate. You might not feel anything in the moment, but later, feelings of sadness or anger can creep in, lingering long after the trigger has passed. This delayed reaction can be just as challenging, as it often leads to misplaced emotions — taking out your frustration on those around you who have nothing to do with your past trauma or the recent event that triggered it. When this happens, it's clear that your past is still holding sway over your present, preventing you from living fully in the here and now.

The truth is, everyone — and every *body* — reacts differently to triggers. But the key to breaking free from their grip is awareness. By becoming aware of your triggers and understanding how they affect you, you can start to control your reactions, rather than letting those triggers control you. The goal is to move beyond your past, so you can live peacefully and confidently in the present moment, unburdened by the weight of old wounds.

In the next section, I'll introduce you to my Trigger to Treasure technique, a transformative method designed to help you turn moments of frustration and emotional turbulence into opportunities for profound growth and self-acceptance. Whether it's an offhand comment from a stranger, a challenging interaction with a loved one, or even a familiar song that brings back painful memories, this technique will empower you to navigate these triggers with grace and resilience. It's about reclaiming your peace and finding your way back to happiness — even in the midst of life's unexpected storms — so that, like me, you can find your own sense of joy and contentment, whether you're in a hammock or anywhere else life takes you.

 The Trigger to Treasure Technique

Follow these four steps to turn your triggers into treasures.

Step 1: Tune In to Your Body

As I mentioned earlier, your brain and body have an incredible ability to remember past events, storing them away in an effort to protect you from similar situations in the future. This instinctual protection mechanism is why it's so important to tune in to your brain and body when a trigger arises. Instead of avoiding or suppressing your reactions, face them head-on with courage and curiosity.

When you notice your body reacting — whether it's a tightness in your chest, tension in your neck, a lump in your throat, or a churning in your stomach — pause and check in with yourself. Ask, "Where am I feeling this trigger?" and identify the sensations. How is your mind reacting? Are thoughts racing through your head like a runaway train, or is your mind going completely blank, shutting down as a form of protection?

Take a moment to truly acknowledge how you feel. Don't shy away from answering yourself honestly:

> I feel like I want to crawl into a cave and hide.
> I feel like I want to scream or punch something.
> I feel like a powerless little kid who isn't allowed to speak up.
> I feel embarrassed and ashamed.
> I feel overwhelmingly sad and desperately lonely.

By identifying where and how you're feeling the trigger, you're taking the first step toward gaining control over it. Recognizing your triggers doesn't just empower you — it allows you to be proactive rather than reactive. Being proactive means you're creating or controlling the situation by taking action before the trigger has a chance to take control. Instead of allowing the trigger to dictate your response, you're taking charge, steering your emotions and reactions with intention and awareness.

Step 2: Take a Breather

Breeeeathe. When you find yourself in a situation where you're being triggered — whether it's by a person, a conversation, or an environment — the best immediate action you can take is to breathe. If you're able to step away and remove yourself from the triggering situation, that's great. But if that's not possible, the next best thing is to breathe through the trigger.

Once you've tuned in to your body and recognized how you feel, start taking deep, slow breaths. A simple technique you can use is called *box breathing*: Inhale deeply through your nose for a count of four, hold that breath for another count of four, exhale slowly through your nose for a count of four, and finally hold for a count of four before inhaling. Repeat this pattern several times. This controlled breathing will help slow down your heart rate, calm your nervous system, and bring you back to the present moment.

Another helpful trick is to place the tip of your tongue at the "fire point," which is located just behind your two front teeth at the ridge of your gum. This small action can help you relax your jaw, neck, face, and shoulders — areas that often tighten up when we're feeling triggered.

The most important thing to remember during this step is to avoid reacting impulsively to your triggers. Reacting in the heat of the moment often means letting the trigger control you, rather than you controlling the trigger. Depending on the intensity of your triggers, you may need to practice this breathing technique multiple times before you can fully understand and manage your reactions.

Some of the most deeply rooted triggers take years — sometimes even decades — to heal. But as the saying goes, "Repetition is the mother of all skill." It takes practice to retrain your brain and body, unlinking those past traumatic events from the present.

The key with step 2 is to simply give yourself a moment of pause. You're not trying to resolve your trigger or eliminate it right then and there — you're just giving yourself permission to breathe through it, to relax into the experience, and to create a little space between you and the intensity of the emotion.

Step 3: Tap into Your Emotions

Just as we spoke about in previous chapters, think of emotion as "energy in motion." Emotions are not meant to be stagnant; they need to flow through you, just like a stream of clear water. When you suppress or ignore your emotions, they become trapped within you, turning murky and stagnant like a puddle of muddy water. Over time, these trapped emotions can build up, leading to stress, anxiety, and even physical ailments. That's why it's essential to pay attention to your emotions and allow them to move freely through your body and mind.

When you recognize that you've been triggered, take a moment to sit with the emotions that arise. It's natural to feel discomfort, frustration, or even embarrassment about being triggered, but there's no shame in it. Triggers are simply messengers, alerting you to unresolved issues from your past. The key is to allow your emotions to surface, acknowledging them without judgment.

One powerful way to process these emotions is through journaling. Grab a notebook and start writing down whatever comes to mind about the triggering moment. Let your thoughts flow freely onto the page, without filtering or censoring them. Ask yourself, *What does this remind me of? How is this triggering event similar to an event in my past?*

As you begin to make connections between the present trigger and past experiences, don't shy away from revisiting those difficult moments. Yes, it may be painful, but it's also a crucial step in the healing process. Take yourself back to that time. How old were you? Who was there? How did you feel during and after the event? What impact did that experience have on your life? Reflect on how that past event shaped your beliefs, behaviors, and patterns.

For example, if a trigger reminds you of a time when you felt powerless as a child, acknowledge that feeling. Perhaps you were criticized by a parent or teacher, and now any form of critique sends you spiraling into self-doubt. By identifying the root cause of your trigger, you can begin to dismantle the power it holds over you.

Look for patterns in your triggers. Do certain situations, words, or people consistently evoke the same emotional response? Understanding these patterns is like uncovering a map of your emotional landscape. Once you can see the paths that lead to your triggers, you can prepare yourself for future encounters, allowing yourself to respond rather than react.

Remember, tapping into your emotions is not about wallowing in the past — it's about understanding and healing. It's about recognizing the emotional baggage you've been carrying and finally setting it down. By confronting your emotions head-on, you're not only processing past pain but also paving the way for a more peaceful and empowered future.

Step 4: Heal the Trigger

Healing your triggers and old wounds is a deeply personal journey, and what works for one person may not work for another. From someone who's spent decades unraveling the threads of past trauma, I can tell you that finding the right key to unlock the treasure hidden within your triggers can be challenging. But is it worth the effort? Oh, absolutely! It's the very process that will set you free to live as your most authentic, happy self. This journey isn't just about emotional healing; it's about nurturing your overall well-being — emotionally, mentally, physically, and spiritually.

If you're embarking on this healing journey on your own, there are many tools and methods available to you. You might dive into self-help books, listen to empowering podcasts, attend retreats that speak to your soul, or engage in practices like yoga, meditation, and journaling. Above all, practicing consistent self-care is crucial. Healing isn't a one-time event; it's an ongoing process of tending to yourself with patience and compassion.

Emotional trauma has a way of snowballing if left unchecked, growing larger and more overwhelming with time. I used to be the queen of turning molehills into mountains, letting small triggers spiral into something much bigger than they needed to be. But with greater self-awareness, I've learned how to prevent those snowballs from gaining momentum in my mind.

It's essential to cut yourself some slack during this process. Remember, you are a human being, and it's natural to have emotional reactions. When you're triggered, your body is simply responding in the way it was designed to — it's a survival mechanism. You were born with emotions, and sometimes being human means riding that emotional roller coaster. Instead of resisting or suppressing these emotions, allow them to flow through you.

As I've shared before, I've faced significant trauma in my life, and some deep-seated wounds continued to trigger me despite my best efforts with self-help practices — they took more than just books, meditation, or yoga could provide. That's when I turned to professional therapy, exploring options like EMDR (eye movement desensitization and reprocessing) and professionally administered ketamine therapy. These therapies were instrumental in helping me process and heal from the trauma that had kept me stuck in a cycle of reactivity.

Whatever path you choose, ensure that you're getting the support you need. Healing isn't just about coping — it's about finding peace in your heart and reclaiming your power. You deserve to be happy, healthy, and whole. That wholeness is the treasure your triggers can yield. It's the gold at the end of the rainbow — the reward for your courage and perseverance.

While we all face tough times, healing from these struggles makes us stronger and more resilient. With each trigger you confront and overcome, you'll find that the next time you're triggered, it doesn't hold the same power over you. The trigger weakens, and you grow stronger. The trigger loses its grip, and you become empowered. That's what I want for you: to find empowerment through your triggers. Let them teach you how to become the next best version of yourself.

Here's a quick recap of the four steps to turn your triggers into treasures:

Step 1: Tune in to your body.
Step 2: Take a breather.
Step 3: Tap into your emotions.
Step 4: Heal the trigger.

Remember, healing is a process — repeat these steps as often as needed until you break free from the cycle of your triggers. You've got this!

Coming Up

As we come to the close of the fifth step to FREEDOM, it's essential to remember the core message: Life isn't just about the destination; it's about savoring every moment of the journey. When we worry too much about what tomorrow might bring, we miss out on the beauty and joy that today has to offer. This step has been all about learning to detach from the need to control every outcome, to embrace the unknown, and to trust in the process. By doing so, you open yourself up to the endless possibilities that life has to offer, and you transform your triggers into treasures.

To deepen your understanding and fully integrate these lessons into your life, I encourage you to take a moment to listen to the Detach from Tomorrow meditation, which corresponds with this step. Let it guide you in embracing the present moment and finding peace in the here and now.

Next, prepare to dive into step 6, where we'll explore how to fully own your badass self and step into your newfound power with confidence. In chapter 14, "Set Healthy Boundaries," we'll delve into the crucial art of establishing boundaries and letting go of the need to please others. As you continue to change and grow internally, your external world will inevitably shift as well. This can sometimes lead to challenges in relationships, as others may struggle to accept the new, empowered version of you.

You'll learn how to create and maintain boundaries that protect your newfound strength and independence. We'll explore the Four D's of Setting Healthy Boundaries, a powerful exercise for boosting your self-esteem, self-worth, and self-acceptance. By *defining*, *deciding*, *declaring*, and *dedicating yourself* to these boundaries, you'll gain the freedom to live life on your own terms, fully embracing the warrior within. Get ready to stand strong in your truth and own your badass self!

STEP

OWN YOUR BADASS SELF

14

SET HEALTHY BOUNDARIES

God, grant me the serenity to accept the things I cannot change,
Courage to change the things I can,
And wisdom to know the difference.
— Serenity Prayer, Reinhold Niebuhr

For most of my life, I struggled with boundaries — not because I didn't know I needed them, but because I was terrified of what might happen if I actually enforced them. Two defining experiences taught me that speaking up for myself was dangerous.

As a little girl, I was abandoned by someone who was supposed to love and care for me. That early wound etched a belief deep into my heart: *My needs don't matter.* I learned to stay quiet, to avoid asking for too much, and to never rock the boat — because if I did, I might be left behind again. That fear of abandonment became a constant companion, whispering that even if I voiced my truth, the price would be losing the people I cared about most.

Then, when I was twenty years old, I finally found the courage to stand up to my boyfriend and speak my truth. The result? He beat the crap out of me. That moment seared a message into my soul: *This is what happens when you stand up for yourself.* So I shrank back into my turtle shell, convinced it was safer to stay small and silent.

From that point on, I lived in fear of disappointing people, causing conflict, or being labeled as "too much." I was terrified that if I prioritized myself, I'd be abandoned all over again. So I said yes when I meant no. I tolerated toxic relationships. I ignored my needs to keep the peace. And I kept placing myself at the very bottom of my own priority list.

Whenever I tried to change or grow, no one celebrated the "new me." They missed the old Wendy — the one who was predictable, easy to manage, and eager to please. Instead of asking others to rise with me, I dimmed my light to keep them comfortable. I crawled back into my shell, again and again.

But one day I realized that not setting healthy boundaries was making me *unhealthy* — physically, mentally, and emotionally. I was exhausted, depleted, and disappearing. I finally became willing to risk losing others in order to stop losing myself.

And that changed everything. Once I embraced the power of honoring my limits, my entire life began to shift.

Disrupting the Familiar

You probably have a grocery store nearby whose layout you know like the back of your hand. You've been there so many times that navigating the aisles feels like second nature. You could practically work there — you know peanut butter is always on the bottom left-hand side of aisle 4, shredded cheddar cheese is nestled beside the eggs in the refrigerated back row, and the all-important coffee is centrally located in aisle 7.

Your grocery shopping routine is almost a ritual. You walk through the sliding glass doors on the left side of the building and make a beeline for the produce section to stock up on fruits and veggies. From there, you weave through the middle aisles, efficiently grabbing your dry goods. Even though they're not on the list, those fresh-baked chocolate croissants in the last aisle always find their way into your cart before you head to the register. Before you know it, you're walking out through the right-side sliding doors, checking your watch and thinking, *Dang! That was fast!*

But then one evening, after a long day at work, you stop by your trusty grocery store to pick up a few ingredients for dinner. You stride through the familiar glass doors, this time grabbing a small basket since you're just picking up a few things. With your purse still slung over your shoulder, you maneuver through the crowd of hurried shoppers and head directly to aisle 9 to grab some taco shells. But when you get there, instead of finding your usual row of taco shells, you're standing in the middle of the toilet paper section.

What in the world? How did I end up here?

You glance up at the sign above your head, certain you're in aisle 9. Yep, it's aisle 9, all right. But where are the taco shells? You scan the aisle, noticing other customers also wandering aimlessly, puzzled expressions on their faces as they try to figure out how they ended up in the wrong place.

Frustrated, you voice your irritation to the other lost and annoyed shoppers, "Dang it! They moved everything around!"

Others quickly chime in, "Oh, I know! I hate when they do this! I came here for salsa, and all I can find is Charmin!"

You join the chorus of complaints, "Why did they have to change everything? It was perfect just the way it was!"

The frustration you feel in the grocery store is a lot like the discomfort that comes with personal change. When the store rearranges its shelves, it disrupts your routine, making it harder to find what you need and leaving you feeling out of sorts. This is a perfect metaphor for what happens in life when we grow or make significant changes. Just as shifting the salsa to a new aisle can throw off your usual shopping rhythm, changes in our lives can unsettle not only ourselves but also those around us.

When you alter your habits, beliefs, or priorities, it can be disorienting for others who are accustomed to the "old you." They may struggle to adjust, feeling like they no longer know how to navigate their relationship with you, just as you struggle to navigate the new layout of the store. Change, even when positive, can create a ripple effect that disrupts the status quo, leading to frustration, confusion, and even resistance from those who were comfortable with how things were before.

Upsetting the Applecart

Let's imagine that when you completed the Wheel of Midlife exercise in chapter 1, you chose to focus on the Health category. Over time, you began making small, positive changes in your daily routine — improving your diet, getting better sleep, and incorporating more movement into your day. While these changes are undoubtedly beneficial for your health and well-being, they might not be seen that way by those around you.

For instance, if your spouse is not on the same path and is content with their current habits, your new lifestyle could be perceived as a threat. Your partner may miss the familiar routine of relaxing on the couch together with potato chips and a Netflix series, rather than adapting to a new routine of steamed broccoli and Zumba classes. Your commitment to improving your life could inadvertently trigger feelings of insecurity or resistance in your partner, leading to tension or disagreements. In this way, by focusing on your own growth, you may unintentionally disturb the balance — unsettling both the proverbial applecart and your spouse.

Here's another example of how your positive changes might negatively impact those around you: Imagine you've lived in the same house, in the same neighborhood, for the past twenty years. It's where you raised your children, hosted countless neighborhood potlucks, and even served as president of the homeowners' association. But now you decide it's time to sell the house — furniture and all — and fulfill your dream of traveling through Europe with just a suitcase and a smile. While this decision fills you with excitement, it may not be met with the same enthusiasm by others.

Your kids, suddenly anxious, might say, "But, Mom, where will we go for the holidays?"

Your best friend, perhaps feeling a tinge of jealousy, could remark, "Must be nice to just take off and travel the world."

The reactions you receive from others may not always align with the support and encouragement you're hoping for as you strive to make positive changes in your life.

Consider divorce, for example. While divorce rates have declined among younger adults, they have increased among those aged fifty and older, with this group accounting for 36 percent of divorces in 2019. Divorce is undoubtedly a significant life change that not only impacts the couple but also ripples out, affecting friends, family, communities, and even the spouses' careers. While society often views divorce through a negative lens, it can sometimes be the right choice for personal growth, well-being, and happiness. This decision, though difficult, might be a crucial step in reclaiming your life and pursuing your true desires, even if it disrupts the expectations and comfort zones of those around you.

Navigating the complexities of your internal world — quieting the negative self-talk, overcoming limiting beliefs, and developing new healthy habits — is a significant challenge under the best of circumstances. However, add the external pressures and judgments from those around you, and this journey toward lasting change can become even more daunting. The opinions, criticisms, and resistance from others often amplify the difficulty, creating additional hurdles that make it harder to stay committed to your path. The external noise can distract and deter you from your goals, making the process of transformation feel like an uphill battle.

Which Path Will You Choose?

When the road gets rough and the weight of external pressures begins to bear down on you, a pivotal decision lies before you: Which path will you choose?

On one hand, you could opt for the easy route. This path involves slipping back into the life you've outgrown, retreating to your old habits, and avoiding the discomfort that comes with change. It's the path of least resistance, where the applecart remains undisturbed and those around you continue to feel comfortable in their familiar roles. But where does that leave you? What happens to your dreams, your growth, and your happiness? Choosing this route means sacrificing your own fulfillment to keep everything and everyone around you in their comfort zone.

On the other hand, you could choose the more challenging route. This path requires courage, perseverance, and a deep commitment to your own well-being. It's a route that might ruffle feathers, shake up the familiar, and lead to some difficult conversations. But it's also the road that leads to your authentic self, where you live a life true to your deepest desires.

As we've explored throughout this book, the journey toward your true self is rarely straightforward. It's filled with obstacles — relationship roadblocks that force you to establish boundaries, financial challenges that test your resilience, and the resurfacing of past traumas that demand healing. The challenging route — the road to freedom — is less traveled for a reason: It's tough. But tough doesn't mean impossible.

Consider the profound insight from Bronnie Ware's book *The Top Five Regrets of the Dying*, where the number one regret is "I wish I'd had the courage to live a life true to myself, not the life others expected of me." This regret serves as a powerful reminder of the importance of choosing yourself, even when the path ahead is difficult.

Reflect on my crossroads moment I mentioned in chapter 1, when I had to decide between continuing down a familiar yet unfulfilling path or daring to take the road toward freedom and fulfillment. Both paths required effort, but only one would lead to the life I truly wanted. I realized that if I was going to put in the work, it might as well be for something that brought me happiness and fulfillment, something that brought me closer to the life I had always dreamed of living.

My road to freedom was fraught with challenges — relationship roadblocks, financial setbacks, and the reopening of old wounds. It's a path that many choose to avoid, preferring instead to settle for less, to turn on their hazard lights and wait for someone to rescue them from discomfort. But you're not like most people. You're a woman waking up to her true potential, igniting her superpowers, and choosing the road to freedom at every crossroads you encounter.

You've come too far to turn back now. Deep down, you know that the effort it takes to navigate this challenging route is worth every step. My hope for you is that you choose this path — the one that leads to your authentic self and your dream life. Yes, it's difficult, and yes, it will require strength, resilience, and an unwavering commitment to yourself. But the rewards — oh, the rewards — are beyond anything you could imagine. This is the path that will allow you to live a life true to yourself, free from the constraints of other people's expectations.

So when the going gets tough and you find yourself at yet another crossroads, I encourage you to remember the journey we've been on together in this book. Remember that the road to freedom is paved with choices — choices that only you can make. And with each choice you make to honor yourself, prioritize your dreams, and stand firm in your truth, you are moving closer and closer to the life you were meant to live.

To ensure a smooth and successful journey toward the life you desire, one of the most crucial tools at your disposal is the ability to set clear, concrete, and consistent boundaries. Boundaries serve as the framework within which you can navigate your relationships and personal growth, helping you protect your energy, time, and emotional well-being. Establishing boundaries is not just about saying no to others; it's about saying yes to yourself and your priorities.

Before we dive into the four essential steps for setting healthy boundaries, it's important to understand why boundaries are necessary, the different types of boundaries, and what a healthy boundary truly looks like.

Why Do You Need Boundaries?

Boundaries are essential for living a life that is truly yours. They are the invisible borders that delineate where your needs, responsibilities, and emotions end and where someone else's begin. Boundaries are not just about keeping others in check; they're about establishing and protecting your sense of self. They allow you to live your life on your own terms, ensuring that you remain true to your values, desires, and priorities.

- **Boundaries define your identity:** Boundaries serve as a powerful declaration of who you are and what you stand for. They help you maintain your identity by clearly communicating what is acceptable and what is not, both to yourself and to others. When you set boundaries, you are essentially saying, "This is who I am, this is what I value, and this is how I choose to live."
- **Boundaries empower you:** People with strong, healthy boundaries tend to have higher self-esteem, greater confidence, and a clearer sense of purpose. Why? Because they prioritize their own well-being. They have the courage to say yes to what nourishes them and no to what drains them. This empowerment comes from knowing that you have control over your life and that you are not at the mercy of other people's demands or expectations.

- **Boundaries reduce stress:** One of the most significant benefits of setting boundaries is the reduction of stress and burnout. When you set clear limits on your time, energy, and emotions, you protect yourself from overcommitment and the emotional exhaustion that comes with it. Boundaries allow you to manage your resources wisely, ensuring that you have enough left for yourself.
- **Boundaries foster healthy relationships:** Healthy boundaries are the foundation of healthy relationships. They create a mutual respect and understanding between you and others, allowing for more genuine and balanced interactions. When you set boundaries, you teach others how to treat you, which can lead to more fulfilling and less conflict-ridden relationships.
- **Boundaries protect your mental health:** Without boundaries, you are more likely to be taken advantage of, manipulated, or overwhelmed by the demands of others. This can lead to feelings of resentment, anger, and sadness, as you constantly feel like you're giving more than you're receiving. Boundaries help you protect your mental health by ensuring that your needs are met and that you are not overextending yourself.
- **Boundaries encourage personal growth:** By setting boundaries, you give yourself the space to grow and evolve. Boundaries allow you to explore new opportunities, take risks, and pursue your passions without the fear of being held back by the expectations of others. They give you the freedom to live a life that is authentic and true to who you are becoming.

In short, boundaries are the key to living a life that feels fulfilling and true to who you are. They are not about shutting people out; they are about ensuring that you have the space and energy to live your life in a way that feels right for you. Without boundaries, you risk losing yourself in the demands and expectations of others, leading to a life that is not truly your own. So it's time to say no to what doesn't serve you and yes to the life you want to create. Boundaries are your path to empowerment, well-being, and true happiness.

Types of Boundaries

Boundaries aren't one-size-fits-all. There are different types of boundaries for different areas of your life, each serving a unique purpose to protect your well-being and ensure your relationships remain healthy and balanced. Generally, these boundaries fall into five main categories: family, friends, romantic relationships, coworkers, and strangers. But let's not forget those everyday interactions that don't fit neatly into a category, like the Starbucks barista who better get your grande latte just right — because yes, that counts as a boundary too!

- **Family boundaries:** Family dynamics can be complicated, often requiring the most nuanced and challenging boundary-setting. These boundaries are crucial because, unlike other relationships, family ties are typically lifelong. Setting boundaries with family members might involve limiting the amount of time you spend together, deciding what topics are off-limits during conversations, or establishing how much influence they have over your personal decisions. Healthy family boundaries allow you to maintain a sense of individuality while still being a part of the family unit.
- **Friendship boundaries:** Friends are the family we choose, but that doesn't mean these relationships are free from the need for boundaries. Friendship boundaries might involve

defining the level of emotional support you're able to give and receive, ensuring that time spent together is mutually fulfilling, and setting expectations around communication. For instance, you might need to set a boundary if a friend is overly dependent on you for emotional support, which can lead to burnout.

- **Romantic relationship boundaries:** Boundaries in romantic relationships are essential for maintaining respect, trust, and mutual understanding. These might include boundaries around personal space, time spent together versus time spent apart, and communication styles. Setting clear expectations about what you need emotionally and physically from your partner can prevent misunderstandings and ensure both of you feel valued and respected.
- **Workplace boundaries:** In a professional setting, boundaries are key to maintaining a healthy work-life balance and ensuring that your job doesn't overwhelm your personal life. These might include setting limits on your availability outside of work hours, defining the scope of your responsibilities, and establishing how you prefer to communicate with colleagues and supervisors. It's also about protecting yourself from workplace toxicity, whether that's in the form of gossip, unrealistic demands, or inappropriate behavior.
- **Stranger and acquaintance boundaries:** Even in brief interactions with strangers or acquaintances, boundaries are important. These are the boundaries that keep you safe and ensure that casual encounters don't infringe on your personal space or well-being. Whether it's a stranger who stands too close in line at the grocery store or a fellow PTA mom who overshares personal details at a school event, knowing how to set clear, polite boundaries can keep these interactions comfortable and respectful.

 The Four D's of Setting Healthy Boundaries

It's clear that boundaries will vary depending on the relationship and the context. Your boundaries with your spouse will look very different from those with your barista — unless, of course, you're married to the barista, in which case you've got a whole different set of boundaries to manage! The key is to tailor your boundaries to suit the relationship and situation, ensuring that you protect your well-being and maintain healthy, fulfilling interactions across all areas of your life.

Step 1: Define Your Boundaries

Let's dive into the foundation of setting boundaries: defining them. This step is crucial because it sets the stage for all the other steps and ultimately leads to higher self-worth, and a happier, healthier you!

What Does It Mean to Define Your Boundaries?

Defining your boundaries means getting crystal clear on what you will and will not tolerate in your life. This clarity is essential across all your relationships — whether with family, friends, romantic partners, coworkers, or even strangers. Take a moment to reflect on each of these five categories, and answer the following questions in your journal.

- **Family:** What behaviors or comments are unacceptable from your family members? For example, is there a recurring criticism from a parent that leaves you feeling inadequate?
- **Friends:** Are there certain actions from your friends that drain you emotionally or physically? Maybe it's a friend who frequently cancels plans last-minute or one who always talks about herself without listening to you.

- **Romantic relationships:** What are your nonnegotiables in a romantic relationship? This could include emotional neglect, lack of respect, or even smaller issues like not communicating affectionately.
- **Coworkers:** How do you want to be treated at work? Perhaps you need to establish boundaries around your time, especially if a colleague tends to interrupt you while you're deep in work.
- **Strangers:** What interactions with strangers make you uncomfortable? For instance, do you need to set boundaries around how you expect to be treated in public spaces or online?

The Circle Boundary Exercise

To help define these boundaries, try the Circle Boundary exercise. Draw a circle on a piece of paper. Inside this circle, write down everything that makes you feel secure, happy, and loved. These are your "yes" factors — the behaviors, actions, and feelings that you want to promote in your life. For instance:

- When my husband kisses me goodnight before we go to sleep.
- When my kids send me a random text just to say hi or share something fun.
- When my friends call to check in on me, simply to see how I'm doing.
- When my coworker respects my time and space by not interrupting me during focused work.
- When my partner gives me a hug or holds my hand without needing to say anything.
- When I receive a compliment that feels genuine and heartfelt.
- When a family member supports my decisions without judgment or criticism.

- When my close friend listens to me fully, offering empathy and understanding without interrupting.
- When someone respects my personal space, physically and emotionally.
- When a colleague acknowledges my contributions at work, showing appreciation.
- When my partner surprises me with small gestures of love, like a note or a cup of coffee.
- When I enjoy quiet time alone to recharge, without feeling guilty about needing personal space.
- When a stranger smiles or offers a kind gesture, such as holding the door open.
- When a friend follows through on plans we made, respecting my time and commitment.

On the outside of the circle, write down everything that brings you stress, frustration, or discomfort. These are your "no" factors — the things you want to eliminate or protect yourself from. Examples might include:

- When someone criticizes or belittles me, especially in front of others.
- When my partner neglects to show affection or doesn't communicate openly.
- When my friend cancels plans last-minute without a valid reason or consideration for my time.
- When a coworker interrupts me during work or piles on tasks without asking.
- When a family member brings up past mistakes or makes negative comments about my life choices.
- When someone disregards my personal space, making me feel uncomfortable.
- When a friend monopolizes conversations without asking how I'm doing or listening to my concerns.

- When I'm pressured into doing something I'm not comfortable with, such as socializing when I need alone time.
- When people invade my boundaries online with unsolicited messages or comments.
- When a stranger is rude or disrespectful by cutting in line or making inappropriate remarks.
- When my partner dismisses my emotions or makes me feel invalidated.
- When family members or friends make assumptions or judgments about my choices without listening to my side.
- When someone fails to acknowledge my contributions at work or takes credit for my ideas.
- When I'm pressured to stay late at work or respond to nonurgent messages outside of working hours.
- When someone tries to guilt-trip or manipulate me into doing something I don't want to do.

You might notice that the outside of your circle is more crowded than the inside. That's a good thing because it means you have a lot of potential for growth. This exercise helps you visualize what you need to keep in your life and what you need to keep out. The goal is to make the inside of your circle so rich with love, joy, and good energy that it becomes a big, beautiful, bloated bubble of bliss — overflowing with everything that lifts you up and leaving no room for what weighs you down.

Where Do You Need Boundaries?

Once you've completed this exercise, take a moment to reflect on the relationships in your life that need strengthening. In your journal or your *Women Waking Up Playbook*, write down the top three relationships or situations where new boundaries need to be set. For each of those, answer the following questions:

- What needs to change in these relationships?
- What boundary do I need to establish to protect my well-being?
- How will this new boundary contribute to a more joyful and peaceful life?

This is your blueprint for building healthier, more fulfilling relationships. The process starts here, with a clear definition of what you need and deserve. Remember, you're creating a protective space for your well-being — an unbreakable bubble of bliss where you can thrive.

With step 1 in place, you're well on your way to setting boundaries that reflect the best version of you. Let's move forward with confidence!

Step 2: Decide

Once you've defined your boundaries, it's time to decide what actions you will take if those boundaries are crossed. This step is crucial because it prepares you to respond assertively and confidently when someone oversteps the line. It's not just about drawing the boundary; it's about enforcing it.

Why Is This Step Important?

Deciding on the consequences ahead of time ensures that you're not caught off guard when someone disrespects your boundaries. Without a plan, you might find yourself unsure of how to respond, which can lead to frustration, resentment, and even the erosion of your self-esteem. By deciding in advance how you will handle boundary violations, you empower yourself to maintain control of your life and relationships.

Crafting Your Plan of Action

Consider the different scenarios in which your boundaries might be crossed in the three relationships or situations you identified in step 1. The consequences you set will depend on the boundary, the relationship, and the specific situation. Here are some examples to guide you:

- **Let it slide the first time?** Sometimes, you might choose to let a minor boundary violation go, especially if it's the first time. For example, if a friend accidentally interrupts you during a conversation, you might decide to overlook it this time, especially if it's out of character for them. However, be mindful that repeated boundary-crossing behavior should not be tolerated.
- **Three strikes, you're out?** In some cases, you might implement a "three strikes" rule. For instance, if a coworker repeatedly disrespects your work-life balance by contacting you after hours, you might decide to give them two warnings before escalating the situation to HR or setting firmer boundaries.
- **End the relationship?** There are times when repeated boundary violations, especially in close relationships, might lead you to end the relationship altogether. For example, if your partner continually criticizes your weight or appearance, makes jokes at your expense, or shames you for expressing emotions despite numerous discussions, it might be time to reassess the relationship.

Creating Your "If This Happens..." List

To solidify this step, create an "If this happens..." list. This list will outline your specific responses to potential boundary violations. For instance:

- **If my friend talks over me:** I will calmly say, "I wasn't finished speaking. Please let me complete my thought."
- **If my boss calls me while I'm on vacation:** I will not answer, and I will send a polite email reminder about my time off once I'm back at work.
- **If my dad criticizes my parenting skills:** I will firmly tell him, "I appreciate your concern, but I'm comfortable with the choices I'm making as a parent. Please keep your parenting opinions to yourself."

This list is your blueprint for action. It gives you a sense of control and clarity, ensuring that you're ready to respond in a way that honors your boundaries and maintains your self-respect. This is a crucial step in owning your badass self.

Step 3: Declare

After defining your boundaries and deciding on the consequences if they're crossed, the next step is to declare those boundaries to the people in your life. Simply knowing your boundaries and writing them down isn't enough; you need to communicate them clearly and assertively. If others aren't aware of your boundaries, they can't respect them, and you'll continue to find yourself in situations where your limits are tested. That said, timing matters. You don't need to initiate a serious conversation out of the blue if everything is going smoothly in a relationship. Instead, wait until a boundary is actually being tested — then speak up with clarity and calm. This approach ensures that your message is timely, relevant, and rooted in real-life situations, which increases the chances that it will be received and respected.

Why Declaring Boundaries Is Essential

Declaring your boundaries is about more than just drawing lines; it's about standing up for yourself and ensuring that others understand

and respect your limits. This is your chance to voice your values, needs, and desires. It's about showing respect for yourself and, in turn, teaching others how to respect you.

The act of declaring your boundaries can feel intimidating, especially when it involves people close to you. You might worry about their reactions or fear that you'll come across as confrontational. But remember, stating your boundaries isn't about starting a conflict; it's about creating clarity and fostering healthier relationships.

How to Declare Your Boundaries

It's crucial to approach these conversations with clarity and calmness. You don't need to yell, shout, or be aggressive to be heard. In fact, the most effective boundary-setting happens when you express yourself clearly, calmly, and confidently.

For example, let's say your coworker, John, has a habit of making sarcastic comments about you during meetings, and it really gets under your skin. The next time it happens, take a deep breath and assertively say, "John, I don't appreciate those comments, and I find them disrespectful. I'd like you to stop."

There's no need for drama or an outburst. By staying calm, you keep control of the situation and make it clear that your boundary is nonnegotiable. If John crosses the line again, you'll be prepared to follow through with the further consequences you decided on in step 2.

The Power of Clear Communication

Declaring your boundaries is also about enhancing your communication skills. When you clearly articulate what you will and won't accept, you make it easier for others to understand and respect your needs. This kind of assertive communication not only strengthens your relationships but also boosts your self-confidence and sense of self-worth.

Remember, the goal isn't to force others into submission but to create mutual understanding and respect. When people are aware of your boundaries, they're more likely to honor them, leading to more harmonious and fulfilling relationships.

A Ripple Effect of Respect

As you continue to declare your boundaries, you'll notice a ripple effect: People will start to treat you with more respect, and your relationships will begin to reflect the healthier dynamics you're cultivating. Over time, you'll waste less energy dealing with frustrations and more time enjoying the things that truly matter to you.

In declaring your boundaries, you're not just drawing lines — you're setting the stage for a life where your well-being is prioritized, your values are honored, and your relationships are built on a foundation of mutual respect. This is where the magic happens, where your blissful bubble starts to grow and your life becomes more aligned with your true self.

Step 4: Dedicate

Once you've defined, decided on, and declared your boundaries, the final and most crucial step is to dedicate yourself to upholding them. This dedication is not just about enforcing boundaries; it's about committing to your own happiness and well-being. It requires consistency, resolve, and the inner strength to stand by the boundaries you've set.

Why Dedication Is Key

Without dedication, boundaries are meaningless. If you draw your boundaries with a pencil — soft, tentative, and easy to erase — others will quickly learn that your limits can be crossed without consequence. They'll see that your words don't match your actions, and your boundaries will be easily dismissed.

Consider this scenario: Judy tells her friend Lisa that she dislikes when people are late. But each time Lisa shows up late, Judy lets it slide. Over time, Lisa begins to see Judy's boundary as inconsequential, something she doesn't need to respect. Judy's boundary, drawn in pencil, is slowly erased with every instance of Lisa's tardiness.

Now imagine a different Judy, one who has drawn her boundaries in permanent marker. When Lisa shows up late again, Judy doesn't just shrug it off. Instead, she calmly but firmly says, "Lisa, if you can't respect my time, we won't be able to make plans anymore." This Judy means business, and Lisa quickly learns that Judy's boundaries are not to be trifled with.

How to Dedicate Yourself to Your Boundaries

Dedication starts with a commitment to yourself. It means that once you've established your boundaries, you uphold them, no matter how challenging it might be. Here's how to do it:

- **Stay consistent:** Consistency is crucial. If you enforce your boundaries one day but let them slide the next, you send mixed signals. Make sure you are consistent in upholding your boundaries every single time they are tested.
- **Be prepared for pushback:** Understand that not everyone will appreciate your boundaries, especially at first. Some people might resist, push back, or try to guilt you into reverting to old ways. Stand firm in your decision, knowing that those who truly care about you will respect your need for boundaries.
- **Hold yourself accountable:** It's easy to let things slide, especially when dealing with close friends or loved ones. But remember, every time you allow a boundary to be crossed without consequence, you undermine your own self-worth. Hold yourself accountable to the standards you've set.
- **Remind yourself of the benefits:** Whenever you're tempted

to let a boundary slide, remind yourself of the benefits that come with strong boundaries: healthy relationships, reduced stress, greater self-esteem, and a happier, more peaceful life.

- **Adapt as necessary:** While it's important to be firm, it's also important to recognize when boundaries need to be adjusted. Life is dynamic, and your boundaries may need to evolve over time. Dedication doesn't mean being rigid; it means being committed to what's best for you at any given moment.

The Rewards of Boundaries

By dedicating yourself to your boundaries, you'll start to see profound changes in your life. Relationships will improve as those around you learn to respect your limits. Your self-esteem will grow as you prove to yourself that you are worthy of respect and care. The drama, stress, and frustration that once filled your life will begin to dissipate, making way for greater peace, happiness, and fulfillment.

In the end, setting and upholding boundaries is an act of self-love. It's about valuing yourself enough to demand the respect you deserve from others — and giving yourself the respect you deserve by following through.

So, as you move forward, remember to keep that proverbial permanent marker handy. Use it to draw your boundaries with confidence and clarity, knowing that by doing so, you're crafting a life that honors and uplifts the very best version of you.

A Quick Review of the Four Steps to Setting Healthy Boundaries

1. **Define:** Start by defining boundaries for every relationship in your life — whether it's with your family, friends, partner, coworkers, or strangers. Identify what you will and

will not tolerate in terms of physical, emotional, sexual, spiritual, and financial interactions. Use the circle exercise to determine what behaviors and actions make you feel secure and respected, and what crosses the line.

2. **Decide:** Once your boundaries are defined, decide what actions you'll take if someone crosses them. Your response may vary depending on the boundary, the relationship, and the situation, but having a clear plan in place is essential. Decide in advance whether you'll address the issue directly, allow for a grace period, or take more definitive action.
3. **Declare:** Clearly communicate your boundaries to the people in your life. Simply having boundaries in your mind isn't enough — you need to vocalize them. Be proactive in expressing your values, needs, and desires, especially in your closest relationships. The more clearly you declare your boundaries, the more likely others are to respect them.
4. **Dedicate:** Finally, dedicate yourself to upholding your boundaries. This means being consistent and following through on what you say. Draw your boundaries with a permanent marker, not a pencil, and enforce them calmly, clearly, and confidently. This dedication ensures that your boundaries are respected and your well-being is prioritized.

Coming Up

Here at the end of step 6, I hope you've discovered the power of setting boundaries and embracing your true self. Remember, owning your badass self means standing firm in your values, protecting your energy, and ensuring that your well-being is prioritized in every relationship and interaction. The boundaries you've established are the pillars of your new, empowered life — guard them fiercely and confidently.

Before you move on, I encourage you to listen to the Own Your Badass Self meditation available in the FREEDOM Meditation Series at WomenWakingUp.com. It will help reinforce the boundary-setting process, solidify your newfound strength, and deepen your commitment to living a life that's true to you.

Now that you've laid the foundation for a life of freedom, authenticity, and strength, it's time to take the final step: Master Yourself. In the next chapter, "Unfunk Yourself," you'll learn how to quickly bounce back when life throws you a curveball. Because let's be real — no matter how empowered you are, shit still happens. And the key is not letting those bad moments spiral into funks that hold you back.

I'll share with you my personal toolkit of nine powerful strategies to help you overcome a bad day so you can get back to rocking your midlife with confidence and joy. Get ready to master the art of resilience, and remember — you've got this!

STEP

MASTER YOURSELF

15

UNFUNK YOURSELF

You may have to fight a battle more than once to win it.
— attributed to Margaret Thatcher

At this point in your journey, you've done some incredible work. You've freed yourself from past limitations, reclaimed your power, envisioned a bold new future, experimented and explored new possibilities, learned to live in the present moment, and fully owned your badass self. What could possibly be left? Now it's time to make sure all that hard work sticks. Welcome to the final stage of your transformation: step 7, "Master Yourself."

Mastering yourself means ensuring that the new, empowered version of you is here to stay, and that the old you — along with all the self-doubt, limiting beliefs, and unhealthy patterns — doesn't resurface. The reality is, life is unpredictable. No matter how much progress you've made, there will be days when things don't go as planned. You could be cruising along the road to freedom, feeling on top of the world, and then — *bam!* — you hit a pothole and find yourself swerving into a ditch. What now?

If you stay in that ditch too long, you risk falling back into old habits and mindsets. This can lead to feelings of sadness, hopelessness, anxiety, depression, anger, frustration, and overall funkiness — a state of mind that can threaten to undo all the progress you've made. The old you might start creeping back in with her outdated thoughts, behaviors, and beliefs. But not on my watch!

In this chapter, I'm going to arm you with a powerful set of tools — nine, to be exact — that will help you bounce back quickly from any bad day and keep you rocking your midlife journey. Instead of calling for outside help when you hit a rough patch, you'll call on the most important person in your life: you. These tools will empower you to rescue yourself — to lift yourself out of the ditch and get back on the road to freedom, stronger and more resilient than ever before. Let's get started!

The Nine Tools for Unfunking Yourself

I gathered these nine tools after navigating my own share of potholes during my midlife awakening. Notice I said *awakening* and not *crisis*. For me, midlife wasn't about crisis; it was about waking up to my true self and making the choice to stay awake — to stay present and intentional with my life. After years of pulling myself out of one ditch after another, I finally learned how to become my own tow truck. I developed strategies to unfunk myself whenever I felt the pull of negativity or overwhelm. Now if I even sense myself getting close to that solid white line, I slow down, grab one of these tools, and get back on track before I veer too far off course.

Yes, even a midlife awakening can bring its share of rough days. While transforming your life is thrilling and full of potential, the process of change can also be challenging and uncomfortable. Life happens, shit happens, and yes, potholes happen. It's all part of being human.

So let's open up your brand-new toolbox and explore what's inside. Some of these tools may seem almost too simple to be effective, but don't be fooled — when practiced consistently, these strategies can make a profound difference in how you manage your moods and maintain control over your life. They enable you to stay on the road to freedom, no matter what challenges come your way.

Tool #1: Be a Kindness Control Freak

This tool is perhaps the most crucial of them all, but it can also be the hardest to master. When you're feeling low, it's all too easy to treat yourself poorly, feeding into negative thoughts, which only deepens the cycle of feeling like crap.

I've mentioned this before, and I'll emphasize it again: Your mind can either be your best friend or your worst enemy. You have the power to decide which voice dominates inside that precious head of yours. You are in control of your thoughts, and if you're going to be a control freak about anything, this is where it counts.

I get it — thinking positively when you're in a funk feels like trying to swim upstream against a strong current. But here's the thing: You have to dig deep and start sprinkling some kindness on your negative thoughts. It might feel like trying to grow flowers in a desert, but with enough persistence, those flowers can and will bloom.

Start by speaking to yourself as your best friend would speak to you. Think about it — your best friend wouldn't tear you down when you're already feeling bad. They wouldn't say:

"I can't believe you put yourself in this situation again."
"Can you do anything right?"
"You are absolutely pitiful."
"What a loser."

If your best friend does speak to you like this, then it's time to find a new best friend! A true friend would say:

"Hey girl, it's gonna be okay."
"You are strong and resilient, and you will get through this."
"Hang in there!"
"You are loved and beautiful."

"Just take a deep breath, relax, and let go."

"I've got your back. I will take care of you."

"I love you."

Doesn't that sound better? More importantly, doesn't that feel better?

Now let's put this into practice. Grab a pad of sticky notes and write out some positive affirmations — things like "I am strong," "I am worthy," or "I am enough." Place these sticky notes on your mirror, your nightstand, your refrigerator, your car dashboard, or your desk. Read them over and over again until those positive affirmations stick in your mind like glue.

Remember, kindness isn't just something you offer to others; it's something you must give to yourself, especially when you need it the most. By becoming a kindness control freak, you're reclaiming control over your thoughts and steering them in a direction that supports your well-being and happiness. So go ahead, be relentless in your kindness toward yourself — you deserve it!

Tool #2: Connect with the Right Friends

Remember that popular game show *Who Wants to Be a Millionaire?* One of the lifelines contestants could use was to "phone a friend" if they didn't know the answer to a tough question. Well, life's challenges often feel like tough questions, and sometimes the best lifeline you can use is to reach out to a friend.

When you're stuck in a funk, it's easy to feel isolated and overwhelmed by your thoughts and emotions. But just like on the game show, your friends can be an invaluable resource — they can offer you new perspectives, solutions to your problems, or even just a distraction from your worries. Sometimes all you need is a conversation to lift your spirits or a fun outing to shift your energy.

However, reaching out can be difficult, especially when you're feeling down. You might be tempted to tough it out alone, telling yourself that you should be able to handle it. Trust me, I've been there. I used to pride myself on having it all together, so much so that I resisted asking for help until I was in a full-blown crisis, landing myself in the ER with chronic depression and anxiety attacks.

Don't wait until you're at your breaking point. Be proactive in reaching out to your friends when you start feeling the weight of the world on your shoulders. Even if you don't want to dive into the nitty-gritty details of why you're struggling, that's okay. You don't have to explain everything — sometimes a simple "Can we meet for coffee?" is all it takes.

The goal is to change your environment and your energy. Surrounding yourself with the right friends can shift your mindset from dwelling on what's wrong to focusing on what's good. Your friends can offer fresh perspectives, share a laugh, or simply be there to listen without judgment. They don't have to fix your problems, but by spending time with you, they can help you feel connected and supported, reminding you that you're not alone in whatever you're going through.

And remember, it's not just about reaching out when you're feeling down. Regularly connecting with positive, supportive friends can keep your spirits high and prevent you from falling into a funk in the first place. Make it a habit to surround yourself with people who lift you up and make you feel good about yourself. These are the friends who will help you steer clear of life's potholes and keep you on the road to freedom and fulfillment.

Tool #3: Move Your Body

Whether it's dancing, walking, hiking, cycling, weight training, boxing, skiing, surfing, stretching, or even skipping to the mailbox for that elusive check from Publishers Clearing House (do they still exist?), the key is to move your body! Physical movement is a powerful way to boost your energy, lift your mood, and help you relax and sleep better — exactly what you need to pull yourself out of a funk.

Exercise has been shown to improve mood and decrease feelings of depression, anxiety, and stress. Physical activity produces changes in the parts of the brain that regulate stress and anxiety, and it can increase brain sensitivity to hormones like serotonin and norepinephrine, which help relieve feelings of depression. This is particularly beneficial during times of hormonal changes, such as menopause, when mood fluctuations can be more pronounced.

Now, for those of you who might cringe at the thought of exercise, here's some good news: It doesn't matter how intense your workout is! Studies have shown that exercise benefits your mood regardless of the intensity of the activity. So you don't have to run a marathon or lift heavy weights to reap the mental health benefits.

As a society, we often think of exercise as a way to lose weight, and while that's true, it's important to shift our perspective and see exercise as a way to improve our overall well-being. Moving your body is about enhancing your emotional state just as much as your physical state.

Personally, I'm a big fan of yoga. Yoga is incredibly relaxing and therapeutic, and the best part is that you can do it right in your own home. There are so many levels of yoga, so don't think you need to be a Cirque du Soleil performer to give it a try. Some teachers even offer chair yoga for those who prefer a gentler approach!

And let's not forget about other fun activities that might not even feel like exercise, such as dance lessons, pickleball, bowling, kayaking, or my personal favorite, Hula-Hooping! The point is to do something, anything, that gets your body moving. I promise that moving your body will help you feel better, both mentally and physically.

Tool #4: Eat Healthy Foods

Food is fuel, and food is energy. Just like we discussed in chapter 9, food is the fuel that powers your body — the vehicle that carries you through life. If you're already feeling like crap and you fuel your body with crappy food, it's going to be a real struggle to pull yourself out of the ditch and escape that funk.

Much like how we tend to think self-defeating thoughts when we're feeling down, we also tend to reach for unhealthy foods when we're in a funk. But here's the thing: What you eat has a profound impact on both your physical and mental well-being. It's critical that you choose nourishing foods, especially when you're feeling down in the dumps.

As we covered in chapter 9, incorporating fresh, whole foods into your diet is essential for maintaining health, particularly during midlife and beyond. This is even more important during times of stress. Think of it this way: good food = good fuel = a healthy body = a healthy mind = positive feelings = feeling good!

One of my go-to strategies when I'm feeling down and need a quick pick-me-up is juicing, particularly focusing on vegetable-based juices with minimal fruit. While fruits are nutritious, they also contain a lot of sugar, so it's best to consume those in moderation and in their solid form, rather than as juice.

In my experience, even though I generally eat well, I find that incorporating more vegetables into my diet helps me feel more energized and mentally sharp. Vegetables are generally alkalizing, which helps offset the acidity that can build up in your body and mind, especially during stressful times. If you're in a funk, chances are your thoughts might be a bit on the negative side, and those negative thoughts can contribute to an acidic environment in your body. Remember, everything is energy — including your thoughts — so nourishing your body with alkalizing foods is like feeding your brain and body the positivity it craves.

If you're interested in exploring this further, try googling an alkaline food chart. You'll find lists showing the pH levels of various foods and beverages. On one end of the spectrum, you'll see items with high levels of acidity, such as alcohol, coffee, and red meats, and on the other end, you'll find more alkalizing foods like broccoli, asparagus, and cashews. It's fascinating to see where your regular foods fall on the spectrum. You can even buy pH test strips at a health food store to test your levels. As you incorporate more alkalizing foods into your diet, you'll notice a decrease in your body's acidity and, more importantly, an improvement in your mood!

Tool #5: Walk in Nature

This tool offers a powerful two-for-one benefit by combining the physical activity of moving your body with the mental and emotional rejuvenation that comes from spending time in nature. Why is connecting with nature so important? Because nature has an incredible ability to ground us, calm us, and restore our body, mind, and soul.

When we're feeling down, it's tempting to stay cooped up inside, retreating to the safety and comfort of our homes. This is understandable, especially when the weather isn't exactly inviting. I know firsthand how challenging it can be to motivate yourself to go outside, particularly when living in a place like Chicago during the dead of winter. But it's essential to push yourself to step outside, because that's where the magic happens.

As human beings, we are inherently connected to nature. We're not meant to be confined within four walls all day long. Just like other animals, we function best in our natural habitat. If you kept a tiger in a cage for too long, it would go crazy. Animals need to roam, to be free, to connect with the earth — and we're no different. For most of human history, we spent our time outdoors, gathering food, exploring, and living in harmony with the natural world.

One practice that embodies this connection with nature is the Japanese method known as *shinrin-yoku*, or forest bathing. *Shinrin-yoku* is not about taking a literal bath in the forest, but rather immersing yourself in the sights, sounds, and smells of the natural world. Studies have shown that forest bathing can lower stress levels, reduce blood pressure, and improve overall well-being. It's a mindful practice of walking slowly, breathing deeply, and letting the natural environment wash over you.

So when you find yourself in a funk, embrace *shinrin-yoku* and take a walk in the nearest forest, park, or even tree-lined street. Hug a tree, stroll through the woods, smell the fresh air, and let nature work its wonders on you. If you're in a place where getting outside is challenging — perhaps because of harsh weather — consider planning a weekend getaway to a place where you can immerse yourself in nature and practice forest bathing.

This practice not only gets you moving, but it also reconnects you with the earth, helping to clear your mind, calm your spirit, and elevate your mood. When you plan an outdoor adventure, whether it's a trip out of town or a simple visit to your local park, you give yourself something to look forward to. And having something to look forward to is key to boosting your mood and pulling yourself out of a funk.

So this week, plan to get outside and indulge in a little *shinrin-yoku*. Your body, mind, and spirit will thank you, and you'll find yourself feeling refreshed, rejuvenated, and ready to take on the world.

Tool #6: Meditate

We've touched on the power of meditation multiple times throughout this book, and for good reason: It's one of the most effective tools you can use to unfunk your energy and get back to feeling like your best self. If you're in a funk, chances are your energy is low, scattered, or blocked, which only feeds into those negative thoughts and feelings. Meditation is the key to shifting that energy and bringing yourself back into alignment.

Let's break it down: Everything is energy, and that includes your thoughts, emotions, and overall state of being. When your energy is off, you feel off, and this is when the funk sets in. Meditation works by helping you tap into your inner energy, clearing out the mental clutter, and creating space for positive thoughts and healing energy to flow in. It's like rebooting your mind and spirit, allowing you to shift from feeling blah to feeling balanced.

I'm not exaggerating when I say that meditation saved me. It pulled me out of some of the darkest times in my life, and it has the potential to do the same for you. Think of it as a detox for your mind — just as you would eat more vegetables to cleanse and nourish your body, you incorporate meditation to cleanse and nourish your mind. The benefits are profound and far-reaching.

As mentioned in chapter 3, numerous studies have shown that meditation can reduce stress, anxiety, and depression, lower blood pressure, and improve overall well-being. It's not just some woo-woo practice; it's a scientifically backed method for bringing your body and mind back into balance. When you meditate, you're giving yourself the gift of stillness and presence, which allows you to gain clarity, find peace, and reconnect with your true self.

One of the key benefits of meditation is its ability to make you more mindful of how you speak to yourself. Remember tool #1, where we talked about the importance of kindness? Meditation enhances this by making you more aware of the thoughts that run through your mind. You'll start to notice when you're being overly critical or negative, and you'll have the power to shift those thoughts to something more loving and supportive. It's like turning up the volume on your inner cheerleader and turning down the volume on that inner critic.

Meditation doesn't have to be complicated or time-consuming. It can be as simple as sitting quietly for a few minutes each day, focusing on your breath, and allowing your thoughts to settle like sediment in a glass of water. With each breath, you're inviting calm into your mind and body, letting go of the stress, worry, and negativity that have been clouding your energy. The beauty of meditation is that it's a practice you can tailor to fit your needs, whether that's through guided meditations, mindfulness practices, or even just a few minutes of deep breathing in silence.

Incorporating meditation into your daily routine is like giving yourself a daily dose of mental and emotional nourishment. It helps you connect with your inner self, find balance amid chaos, and cultivate a sense of peace that can carry you through even the toughest of times. And when you practice meditation regularly, you'll find that the funk that once felt so overwhelming begins to lose its grip on you. Instead, you'll be better equipped to handle life's challenges with grace and resilience.

Remember, meditation is a powerful skill, and like any skill, it becomes more effective the more you practice it. Start small if you need to and gradually build up your practice. Refer back to chapter 3 for suggestions on different meditation methods, and don't forget to download the FREEDOM Meditation Series for guided sessions tailored to the *Women Waking Up* journey. By making meditation a nonnegotiable part of your life, you'll find that it not only helps you unfunk yourself but also strengthens your overall sense of well-being and empowerment.

Tool #7: Talk to a Therapist

Therapy has been a cornerstone of my journey since I was a teenager. Over the past thirty-five years, I've turned to it whenever I needed an extra boost to navigate life's challenges. If you find the right therapist and the right therapeutic approach, it can be nothing short of life-changing — it certainly was for me. Sometimes the impact of therapy can be felt surprisingly quickly, offering relief and clarity when you need it most.

One of the most powerful aspects of therapy is simply having a space to release what's weighing you down. Emotions like sadness, frustration, depression, or anxiety can feel overwhelming when bottled up inside. But when you articulate those feelings, when you bring them out of your heart and into the open, that heavy load often feels a bit lighter.

For me, talking things out is essential for processing emotions and finding solutions. I'm someone who tends to think out loud, so I'll spend an hour in a session just spilling everything out — my thoughts, feelings, worries — while my therapist listens, nodding along. By the end of the session, I often find myself saying, "Whew! Well, I feel better!" Sometimes all it takes is having someone who provides a safe, nonjudgmental space where you can vent freely and sort through the chaos in your mind.

If you've never tried therapy and feel hesitant, I encourage you to give it a shot. Or perhaps you've had a less-than-stellar experience with therapy in the past. Finding the right therapist and the right type of therapy can involve a bit of trial and error. But trust me, it's worth it when you find the right fit. The relief, insight, and growth that can come from effective therapy are invaluable.

These days, therapy is more accessible than ever. You don't have to go to a physical office; there are plenty of options for remote therapy via videoconference or phone sessions, making it less time-consuming and so much easier logistically.

Whether you're dealing with a major funk or just need a little extra support, therapy can be a critical tool in your toolbox. Sometimes we need more than just a walk in nature, a yoga class, or a glass of green juice to pull us out of a tough spot. And that's okay. Seeking therapy doesn't mean you are weak or don't have your life together — it's about having the courage to get help when you need it and being proactive in your mental and emotional health care. Use every resource available to you to get back on track and stay on the road to freedom and fulfillment.

Tool #8: Watch Funny Movies and Relax

This is my favorite tool of all because laughter truly is the best medicine! When you're feeling down, trying to pull yourself out of that funk can feel like an uphill battle. Sometimes the best thing you can do is take a break from all the "trying." Now, I'm not advocating for escapism or avoiding your problems altogether, but there's a lot to be said for giving yourself a well-deserved break.

Imagine this: You slip into your coziest PJs, make a bowl of buttery popcorn, curl up on the couch, and turn on Netflix. You find a funny movie — something guaranteed to make you laugh until your sides hurt. That little escape might be exactly what you need to lift your spirits. Laughter has this magical ability to shift your energy, lighten your mood, and improve your emotional well-being. Whether it's the ridiculous antics of Austin Powers or the witty banter in *As Good as It Gets*, watching a funny movie might not solve all your problems, but it will definitely give your soul a boost.

It's also important to give yourself permission to relax. I used to be terrible at allowing myself to take a break. Even when I did, I would feel guilty and start thinking about everything I should be doing instead. Don't do that to yourself! Give yourself the space to unwind and just chill out without guilt. Relaxing is not a luxury — it's a necessity, especially when you're trying to unfunk yourself.

If movies aren't your thing (as Austin Powers might say, "This sort of thing ain't my bag, baby"), find something else that makes you laugh, smile, and let go. Check out a comedy club, stream a stand-up special, or binge-watch silly pet videos on YouTube. You could even scroll through Instagram to catch someone doing something hilariously ridiculous.

And speaking of social media, be mindful of your feed. If someone's posts consistently bring you down, it's time to hit "Unfollow." Your emotional environment matters, and that includes both your online world and your personal life. Surround yourself with positivity, whether it's people, content, or experiences.

Tool #9: Ground Yourself

Sometimes life can feel overwhelming, and it's easy to get lost in a whirlwind of thoughts and emotions. When you're in a funk, grounding yourself in the present moment can be the key to regaining control and centering your mind. That's where the 3-2-1 Grounding technique comes in. It's a simple yet powerful tool to help you reconnect with your surroundings and bring your focus back to the here and now.

The 3-2-1 Grounding technique works because it interrupts the cycle of negative or anxious thoughts by refocusing your attention on sensory experiences. This shift in focus can calm your mind, slow your breathing, and help you regain a sense of control over your emotions. It's a quick, accessible tool you can use anytime, anywhere — whether you're at work, at home, or even in the midst of a stressful situation. Ready to try it?

The 3-2-1 Grounding Technique

Step 1: Focus on Three Things You Can See

Start by looking around you and identifying three things you can see. These could be anything in your environment — your coffee mug, a plant on your desk, or the pattern on your carpet. The key is to take a moment to really observe these objects, noticing their colors, shapes, and details. This visual grounding pulls you out of your thoughts and anchors you in the physical world.

Step 2: Tune In to Two Things You Can Hear

Next, close your eyes (if you feel comfortable) and focus on two things you can hear. Maybe it's the hum of your air conditioner, the chirping of birds outside, or the distant sound of traffic. Tuning in to these sounds helps shift your attention away from internal chatter and into the auditory experiences around you, further grounding you in the present moment.

Step 3: Connect with One Thing You Can Touch

Finally, bring your awareness to one thing you can touch. This could be the smooth surface of your desk, the softness of your clothing, or the coolness of a glass of water. By physically engaging with your environment, you complete the grounding process, firmly anchoring yourself in the present.

Whenever you start to feel overwhelmed, anxious, or just out of sorts, take a few moments to go through the 3-2-1 steps. You can even practice this technique regularly, building it into your daily routine as a way to maintain a calm and centered state of mind.

With the 3-2-1 Grounding technique in your toolbox, you have yet another effective strategy to help you unfunk yourself and stay on the road to freedom and happiness. Use it whenever you need a quick reset, and let it bring you back to the present moment with clarity and calm.

Chock-Full of Tools

So there you have it, my little mechanic! You now have your very own toolbox filled with the tools to unfunk yourself whenever life throws you in a ditch. Remember, the quicker you reach for these tools, the quicker you'll recover and get back to living a life you love. Keep that toolbox handy — you never know when you might need it!

Here's a recap of the nine tools:

Tool #1: Be a kindness control freak.
Tool #2: Connect with the right friends.
Tool #3: Move your body.
Tool #4: Eat healthy foods.
Tool #5: Walk in nature.
Tool #6: Meditate.

Tool #7: Talk to a therapist.
Tool #8: Watch funny movies and relax.
Tool #9: Ground yourself.

In this chapter, you've gained a powerful toolkit designed to pull you out of any funk and get you back on the path to joy, fulfillment, and purpose. Whether by connecting with friends, getting lost in laughter, or tapping into the power of meditation, you now have what it takes to quickly bounce back from life's inevitable potholes. Remember, the key to mastering yourself is not about avoiding the ditches but knowing how to climb out of them swiftly. You've empowered yourself with these tools — now you can use them whenever you need a boost.

Coming Up

As we close this chapter on bouncing back, we move into the final, vital step: learning how to *stay* in this newfound freedom, happiness, and strength. In chapter 16, I'll show you how to stay WILD by embracing a philosophy that ensures your life is filled with purpose, passion, and play. You'll discover how to *wake up with gratitude*, *invite more miracles*, *love who you are*, and *drive it home*. Life may be short, but that just means we need to make the most of every moment. Let's commit to living fully, loving deeply, and staying WILD all the way.

Let's dive into the final chapter and ensure that you're living your best, most authentic life.

16

STAY WILD

Life should not be a journey to the grave with the intention of arriving safely in a pretty and well-preserved body, but rather to skid in broadside in a cloud of smoke, thoroughly used up, totally worn out, and loudly proclaiming "Wow! What a ride!"

— attributed to Hunter S. Thompson

One profound insight I've gained through this journey of self-reinvention is that coincidences simply don't exist. The more deeply I have connected with my authentic self and embraced my true purpose, the more the universe has seemed to conspire in my favor. The moment I decided to fully commit to my own path, the universe responded by paving the way for me. Once I wholeheartedly said yes to myself, it was as if a divine force rolled out a red carpet, guiding me forward.

Saying yes to myself didn't magically erase all my doubts. In fact, as I approached my next significant milestone — launching *The Midlife Makeover Show* podcast — my fears and insecurities only grew louder. Despite everything I had overcome in recent years, this new venture felt like the most daunting challenge of all.

As difficult as it had been to live alone in Chicago, endure working long hours to climb out of debt, and confront the darkest corners of my soul, those experiences seemed less intimidating compared to the vulnerability of truly putting myself out there. Oddly enough, staying in a city that never quite felt like home, stuck in a job that didn't fulfill me, had felt safer than the prospect of sharing my voice with the world on my own podcast — a dream that made me feel both wildly excited and completely exposed.

A flood of panic-stricken thoughts rushed through my mind: *Am I really ready to share the intimate details of my life with the entire world? Am I good enough to be a writer and podcaster? Is this the right path, or is it not too late to abandon this wild dream of starting my own show and becoming a writer? Maybe I could just find a remote job and drift across the country doing that instead. That doesn't sound so bad, does it?* With my target launch date looming, I had only a few weeks left to decide if I was truly committed to this bold new venture or if it was time to reconsider everything.

At this point, I found myself savoring the serene atmosphere of Santa Fe so much that I decided to extend my stay by another week. The peaceful environment gave me the space I needed to reflect and contemplate my next steps. Little did I know, fate was about to guide me toward a new opportunity.

As Fate Would Have It...

One cool desert evening, I was grilling a juicy steak and some asparagus on my Coleman grill, enjoying the simple pleasure of cooking outdoors. As I tended to the food, a silver-haired woman strolled by my RV with her golden retriever, a friendly old fellow with a wagging tail and curious eyes.

"Good evening!" she called out, gently tugging on the leash to keep her eager dog from wandering too close. "I think Charlie here can smell that steak from a mile away!"

Her cheerful voice was a welcome break from the solitude I'd been enjoying, so I smiled and replied, "Good evening! He has good taste — this filet mignon is almost ready."

She chuckled and then asked, as many RV park neighbors do, "So, where are you traveling from?"

"Well, I was living in Chicago until recently, but now I'm on the road full-time," I explained, flipping the steak one last time.

Her eyes widened in surprise. "Wow, that's quite the adventure! You must be retired to have all this time to travel."

Laughing, I shook my head. "Not quite! I'm still working — just remotely. All I need is a decent Wi-Fi connection, and I'm good to go."

"Isn't that something," she said with a nostalgic smile. "Back in my day, my husband and I had to wait until he retired from his government job before we could even think about traveling. The freedom you have now is incredible! What kind of work lets you live like this?"

For a moment, I hesitated. This was the first time I'd have to articulate my new identity since leaving behind my corporate career. I decided to embrace it. "I'm a podcaster and writer," I said, the words feeling both strange and exciting as they left my mouth.

Her eyes lit up. "A writer, you say? I've always wanted to write, but I never had the courage to follow that dream. I ended up working at a bank for thirty years instead. Now that I'm in my eighties, it feels like it's too late to start something new."

I placed the steak on my plate and looked up at her, sensing a tinge of regret in her voice. "It's never too late to start," I offered gently. "Even small steps can lead to something wonderful."

She smiled wistfully, pulling Charlie a little closer. "You're right about that. Seeing you chase your dreams is inspiring. Life really is short — better to live it fully."

I topped the steak with a generous pat of butter and returned her smile. "Thank you for saying that. It's a good reminder to keep pushing forward, no matter what."

She nodded, her eyes warm with understanding. "Well, I'll let you enjoy your dinner. My name's Barbara, by the way. My husband,

Albert, and I are just down the way at site 52. If you need anything, feel free to stop by. How long are you staying?"

"Nice to meet you, Barbara. I'm Wendy," I replied. "I think I'll stay a few more days — Santa Fe has a way of making you want to linger."

Barbara's face brightened. "You're right about that. Santa Fe has its own kind of magic. If you have time, treat yourself to a day at Ten Thousand Waves. A soak in the hot tubs and a massage might be just what you need to clear your mind."

"That sounds perfect. I'll definitely check it out," I said as I turned off the grill.

As Barbara and Charlie walked away, I felt a renewed sense of purpose. Maybe it was the calm of Santa Fe or maybe it was the kind words of a stranger, but I knew I was on the right path.

As the sun dipped below the rugged mountains, casting a golden glow across the desert landscape, I felt a deep sense of contentment settle over me. My belly was pleasantly full from the perfectly grilled steak, and the calm of the evening air whispered that it was time to wind down. With a satisfied sigh, I decided to call it an early night. I snuggled under my thick, cozy comforter, feeling its warmth wrap around me like a gentle hug. My little RV bedroom, with its minimalist charm, felt like a sanctuary, even if it did include the world's tiniest nightstand.

Curious about the spa Barbara had mentioned, I reached for my phone and started scrolling through the resort's website. My eyes widened as I took in the pictures — soaking tubs nestled among the pines, serene massage rooms bathed in soft light, and luxurious treatments that promised to melt away stress. *Wow, this place looks incredible*, I thought, feeling a flutter of excitement. The idea of treating myself to a day of pampering sounded too good to resist.

Why not? I decided with a grin. *I deserve this*. Without a second thought, I booked a package that included a revitalizing facial, a soothing massage, and best of all, a private hot tub where I could unwind and let my thoughts drift. Maybe the serene atmosphere would help me sort through the swirling questions in my mind — like whether I was truly ready to embrace the identity of being a "podcaster and writer."

As I set my phone down and nestled deeper into the covers, a sense of anticipation washed over me. Tomorrow wasn't just another day — it was a chance to reconnect with myself, to reflect on this journey I'd embarked on, and to decide whether I was ready to fully step into this new chapter of my life.

Spa Day

With my hair piled high in a loose bun, I shuffled into the spa's serene reception area, feeling both excited and a bit nervous. The plush white robe draped over me felt like a warm embrace, while the soft gray flip-flops made a gentle slapping sound on the polished wooden floor. The air was infused with the calming scent of sage and bergamot, a fragrant blend that immediately set me at ease. The atmosphere was distinctly Japanese, with minimalist decor that radiated tranquility. As I took a seat, I couldn't help but let my mind wander, wondering what this day would bring.

Before long, a soft-spoken woman with a warm demeanor appeared in the doorway. "Wendy Valentine?" she called out, her voice as soothing as the space around us.

I quickly stood up, careful not to trip over the hem of my oversized robe. "Yes, that's me," I replied, stepping forward

She met me halfway, gently placing a hand on my shoulder as she introduced herself. "Welcome to Ten Thousand Waves. I'm Laura," she said, her kindly eyes meeting mine.

As we walked together down a dimly lit hallway, the flickering candlelight casting soft shadows on the walls, I felt a sudden and inexplicable connection to her. It was as if we shared an unspoken bond, a recognition of something familiar that I couldn't quite place. The deeper we ventured into the spa, the stronger this feeling grew. It wasn't just a passing thought — it was a gut instinct telling me that this meeting was more than just a coincidence.

As we stepped into the softly lit massage room, Laura turned to me with a smile. "So, Wendy," she asked, her voice calm and reassuring, "is there any area in particular you'd like me to focus on today?"

I couldn't resist a little humor. "Yes, inside my head!" I quipped, grinning. We both burst into quiet laughter, trying to keep our giggles contained so as not to disturb the tranquil atmosphere of the spa.

Realizing she might take me seriously, I added, "I'm just kidding. My body feels pretty good overall, but honestly, I booked this spa day to clear my mind. I've got some big decisions ahead, and I'm hoping for a bit of clarity."

Laura's interest piqued. "Oh? That sounds intriguing! What kind of decisions?"

Taking a deep breath, I shared, "Well, the past few years have been a whirlwind. After going through a divorce, losing my brother, and hitting rock bottom, I've been rebuilding my life from the ground up. Now I'm traveling the country in an RV, trying to figure out if I have what it takes to be a successful podcaster and writer. I want to help other women who've been through similar struggles."

As I spoke, I noticed Laura's expression change. Her eyes welled up with tears, and she took a moment before responding. "Oh my gosh, Wendy," she said softly, her voice trembling. "I lost my brother last year to addiction, and just last week, I was served with divorce papers after twenty years of marriage."

Her words hit me like a ton of bricks. I was stunned, almost speechless. But I managed to say, "I'm so sorry, Laura. I had a feeling we shared a connection, but I never imagined it would be this profound."

Laura's face softened, and she wiped away a tear. "You're living proof that it's possible to overcome all that pain and still find a way forward. I can't wait to hear your podcast and read your book. Please, hurry up and make it happen — I need some inspiration to get through this!"

In that moment, we both reached out instinctively, embracing each other as if we'd been friends for years. Two women who had started the day as strangers were now bound together by shared experiences of love and loss.

After a long hug, Laura smiled through her tears and said, "But enough about me. You came here to relax, so let's focus on that. Time for your massage."

Waking Up in My Dream

With my face nestled in the cradle of the massage table, I closed my eyes, feeling the warmth of the room envelop me. The gentle chirping of birds outside the window, the soothing scent of sage and bergamot mingling with lavender, and Laura's skilled hands easing the tension from my muscles — all of it transported me to a place of deep relaxation. My thoughts, usually so frantic, began to dissolve like clouds clearing from a bright blue sky.

As I drifted into a peaceful sleep, I found myself in the middle of a bustling hotel lobby filled with laughter, chatter, and the buzz of excitement. Women were gathered everywhere, sipping coffee and discussing the incredible lineup of speakers at a conference. I noticed a long line snaking through the crowd, leading all the way to the stage. Curious, I approached one of the women in line and asked, "What's going on? Who's everyone waiting to see?"

Her face lit up with enthusiasm. "Oh! We're all here to meet this amazing author and get our books signed. She's changed so many lives!" I decided to join the line, eager to meet this inspirational figure.

After what felt like hours of waiting, I finally reached the stage.

The author was barely visible behind a towering stack of books and the eager crowd surrounding her. As the woman ahead of me stepped aside, I moved forward, excited to see who this famous author was.

To my amazement, when I finally reached the table, the author I had been waiting to meet was none other than... *me* — dressed in a vibrant pink dress, holding a matching pink pen. It was surreal, as though I was looking at a future version of myself, full of confidence and success. She smiled warmly as she signed a book and inscribed:

I knew you could do it!
XO,
Wendy Valentine

Then, as she looked up, our eyes met, and with a knowing smile, she said, "Look at all the lives we've changed, Wendy." In that moment, it hit me: The author everyone had been lining up to meet was me, embodying the person I was becoming.

Suddenly, I felt a gentle tap on my shoulder. As I turned around, the dream began to fade. A soft, soothing voice called me back to reality. "Okay, Wendy, that concludes your treatment for today."

Groggy but serene, I blinked my eyes open and whispered, "Wow. I really needed that."

Laura's voice was calm and steady as she asked, "Did you find the clarity you were looking for?"

With a smile, I replied, "Actually, yes, I did. Thank you, Laura. Thank you so much."

That evening, I returned to my cozy RV feeling rejuvenated, both physically and mentally. My body felt lighter, my mind was clear, and for the first time in a long while, I felt a deep sense of purpose. The day at the spa had done more than just relax me — it had opened my eyes to the truth I had been avoiding.

Settling down at my small dinette table, I pulled out my journal and my trusty pink pen. The pages were filled with my thoughts and reflections, but tonight felt different. Tonight I was writing with a renewed conviction. As I penned my thoughts about the day, I realized something important: I had been standing in my own way. By clinging to my doubts and insecurities, I wasn't just holding myself back — I was also preventing other women from finding their strength through my story. If I continued to hide my light, I would be denying others the opportunity to change their lives. It was an inspiring thought.

I wrote about how the spa had brought me to this realization, how it had helped me see that my fears were not just mine — they were shared by many women who needed to hear that they too could overcome. It would be selfish of me to let those fears stop me from shining my light and sharing my journey with the world.

With a sense of calm and determination, I closed my journal. I knew what I had to do. As I curled up in my warm bed, surrounded by the quiet stillness of the night, I whispered a silent thank-you to Barbara at site 52. Her simple suggestion to visit the spa had set off a chain of events that led me to this moment of clarity. It was clear now: My next destination wasn't just a place on a map; it was the launch of my podcast, the start of something bigger than myself.

With that thought in mind, I drifted off to sleep, feeling more certain than ever that I was on the right path.

The Launch

A couple of months after leaving Santa Fe, the universe seemed to conspire in perfect harmony to bring me to this pivotal moment. Not only did the stars align, but so did the numbers on the calendar and the time on the clock. It was 2-22-22 at exactly 2:22 p.m., a date and time I couldn't have planned better if I'd tried. The vibrant California sun cast its warm orange glow over Felisha's roof as we sat perched on a hill at the Malibu Beach RV Park. Below us, the waves of the Pacific Ocean crashed rhythmically against the shore, their steady roar a reminder of the unstoppable force of nature — and the journey I had been on.

As I sat at my small dinette table, I took a deep breath, feeling the significance of the moment settle over me. The ocean, the sun, the date, the time — it all felt like a cosmic nudge, urging me forward. I leaned over my Blue Yeti microphone, the tool that would help me share my voice with the world, and with a mix of excitement and nerves, I spoke the words that had been waiting to be said: "Welcome to *The Midlife Makeover Show*. I'm your host, Wendy Valentine."

In that instant, everything felt right. The doubts and insecurities that once held me back were now just a whisper in the background, replaced by a newfound confidence and purpose. This was more than just the launch of a podcast; it was the start of a new chapter in my life, one where I could finally shine my light and help others do the same.

How to Stay WILD

Since that fateful day, I've recorded nearly three hundred podcast episodes, interviewing an incredible cast of midlife superheroes. In the process, the universe revealed one more life-changing tool to me: my Stay WILD philosophy. I'll now share that philosophy to show you how to *wake up with gratitude*, *invite more miracles*, *love who you are*, and *drive it home*. Whether you're reinventing yourself, pursuing a dream, or simply trying to navigate the twists and turns of midlife, this framework will guide you toward living your most authentic and empowered life.

Wake Up with Gratitude

Prince begins his iconic song "Let's Go Crazy" with the line, "Dearly beloved, we are gathered here today to get through this thing called life." I think we need a little twist on that sentiment. As much as I adore Prince — and believe me, as his number one fan, I do — I suggest we adjust that line to say, "to *thrive* through this thing called life."

Because let's face it, just getting through life isn't enough. *Getting through* implies survival, mere existence, or hanging on by a thread. It's like trudging along with your head down, hoping to make it to the end without too many scars. But *thriving* — that's a whole different story. Thriving means embracing life with open arms, finding joy in the everyday moments, and living fully within this brief blink of time we have in eternity. Thriving is about waking up each day with a heart full of gratitude, ready to take on whatever comes our way.

Whenever I catch myself sinking into self-pity or struggling to appreciate life, I can't help but think of my ex-husband, Jason. As you know, Jason tragically passed away in his sleep at the tender age of twenty-six. Reflecting on that loss always brings a wave of perspective crashing over me. At the time of writing this, I am fifty-two years old — exactly twice the age Jason was when his life was cut short. When I think about that, I'm humbled, even embarrassed, by the moments when I've allowed myself to be ungrateful for the incredible gift of time I've been given.

Jason never had the chance to experience the magical midlife years, to watch his son grow into the remarkable man he is today, or to embrace more of life's joys and challenges. He missed out on so many of the ordinary and extraordinary moments that come with adulthood — a privilege that so many of us take for granted. The thought of this stirs a deep sense of gratitude within me, not just for the bright days but for the difficult ones too. After all, every single moment — whether filled with laughter or tears — is part of the richness of life.

So here I am, fifty-two years into this journey, and I feel deeply thankful. Thankful for the ups and downs, for the smiles and the frowns, and for every experience, past, present, and future. I'm honored to have the opportunity to continue living on this beautiful planet, and I carry Jason's memory as a constant reminder to cherish every moment, no matter how small or challenging.

Just as I can't hand you a jar filled with courage to pursue your dreams, I also can't make you feel gratitude for your life. Gratitude isn't something that can be given; it must be cultivated from within. My hope is that as you've journeyed through the pages of this book, you've begun to recognize and appreciate your own magnificence. I hope you feel inspired to fill up your own metaphorical jar of courage with each amazing feat you accomplish in the years to come.

Incorporating gratitude into your daily life doesn't require a fancy journal or elaborate rituals — though those can be helpful tools. What it truly requires is a commitment to investing in your life with intention and love. When you nurture yourself, you're also nurturing the gratitude that will naturally flow from a life lived with purpose and awareness. The more you light up your own life, the more you illuminate the lives of those around you. Gratitude becomes a ripple effect, spreading joy and positivity far beyond your own experience. It's a win-win for everyone.

So here's a simple challenge for you: When you wake up tomorrow and open your eyes, take a moment to be truly thankful. Grateful that you've been given another day, another chance to thrive through this thing called life. Let that gratitude set the tone for your day, guiding your thoughts, actions, and interactions with others.

Tips for Cultivating Gratitude Daily

- **Start with a morning mantra:** Before your feet hit the floor, take a deep breath and mentally repeat a simple mantra like *I am grateful for this day and all it will bring.* This sets a positive tone and focuses your mind on the good from the very start.
- **Practice mindful appreciation:** Throughout your day, pause occasionally to notice and appreciate the small things — a

warm cup of coffee, a smile from a stranger, the sound of birds chirping. Mindfulness enhances your awareness of the abundance already present in your life.

- **Express gratitude to others:** Make it a habit to thank the people in your life. Whether it's a quick text, a handwritten note, or simply saying "thank you" more often, expressing gratitude strengthens your relationships and spreads positivity.
- **Reflect on challenges with gratitude:** When you face difficulties, try to reframe them. Ask yourself, *What can I learn from this?* or *How is this experience helping me grow?* Finding the silver lining helps transform challenges into opportunities for growth and gratitude.
- **End your day with reflection:** Before you go to sleep, ask yourself, *What was my favorite moment of the day?* This simple question encourages you to mentally scan through your day, focusing on positive experiences. This practice helps shift your mindset toward gratitude, allowing you to end your day on a peaceful, positive note.

Remember, gratitude is a powerful force that can transform your life from the inside out. It's about more than just acknowledging the good; it's about fully embracing the journey, with all its highs and lows. As you move forward, let gratitude be your guide, your anchor, and your source of light in this beautiful adventure called life.

Invite More Miracles

I'll be honest — I've never been one to memorize Bible verses or recite scripture by heart. But there's one verse that has always resonated with me deeply, and that's Matthew 7:7–8: "Ask and it will be given to you; seek and you will find; knock and the door will be opened to you. For everyone who asks receives; the one who seeks finds; and to the one who knocks, the door will be opened."

This verse is particularly fitting for this section on inviting more miracles into our lives. It serves as a powerful reminder that sometimes all we need to do is ask. While it's important to work hard and pursue our goals with determination, we must also remember to pause and look up, to reach out and ask for the guidance, support, or opportunities we need. The universe is not indifferent to our desires; it's a loving force that's ready and willing to assist us on our journey of transformation. All we need to do is trust, ask, and be open to receiving.

As we discussed back in chapter 3, "Become Your Own BFF," everything in existence is energy — our bodies, the chair you're sitting on, the lamp across the room, even the tree swaying gently outside your window. We're all interconnected, floating together in this vast, vibrant cosmic soup. When we ask, seek, and knock, we're tapping into that energy, setting into motion forces that can bring about the changes we desire.

So as you move forward, don't hesitate to ask for what you need, whether it's clarity, courage, resources, or even a little miracle. Remember that the universe is listening, and it's ready to help you pave the way toward your wildest dreams.

To invite more miracles into your life, here are five powerful practices that will help you ask, seek, and knock on the door of your dreams. Each of these tools is designed to help you connect with your inner wisdom, align with the energy of the universe, and open yourself to the abundance that's waiting for you.

Practices for Inviting Miracles

- **Meditation: connecting with your inner voice.** Start your day with a few minutes of quiet meditation. Focus on your breath, allowing your mind to settle. Once you feel calm, silently ask the universe for guidance or clarity on something you're working toward. Picture your desires as already fulfilled, and allow yourself to feel the gratitude and joy that come with that realization.

- **Mindfulness: paying attention to signs.** Throughout your day, practice mindfulness by paying attention to the world around you. Notice any signs or synchronicities that may serve as answers to your questions or desires. Whether it's a chance encounter, a repeating number, or a sudden inspiration, being mindful allows you to recognize when the universe is responding to your asks.
- **Prayer: asking with faith.** Incorporate a simple prayer into your daily routine. This can be a traditional prayer or simply a heartfelt conversation with the universe, God, or whatever higher power you connect with. Ask for what you need — whether it's strength, wisdom, or support — and trust that your request is being heard.
- **Visualization: knocking on the door of possibility.** Visualization is a powerful way to knock on the door of your dreams. Spend a few minutes each day visualizing your goals as if they have already come to pass. Imagine the details vividly — what you see, hear, feel, and experience. This mental practice not only boosts your confidence but also aligns your energy with the outcome you desire.
- **Affirmations: reinforcing your requests.** Use affirmations to reinforce your desires. A statement like *I am open to receiving all the good the universe has to offer* or *The universe is guiding me toward my highest good* can be repeated throughout the day to keep your mindset positive and focused.

By integrating these practices into your daily life, you're actively engaging in the process of asking, seeking, and knocking. These tools help you to stay connected with the energy around you, ensure you're in tune with your desires, and open the door for miracles to unfold. Remember, the universe is ready and waiting to support you — you just need to ask.

Love Who You Are

No matter how many candles you've added to your birthday cake over the years, one thing is certain: You've already undergone countless changes, both inside and out. Remember those days when your younger self could stay up all night and still bounce back without missing a beat? Now, as you navigate midlife, the thought of interrupted sleep thanks to a midnight bathroom run can feel like a major disruption. Just as your body, mind, and spirit have evolved over the decades, they will continue to do so as you journey into your sixties, seventies, eighties, and beyond.

Aging brings inevitable changes, some of which may be less than welcome. Wrinkles start to appear, your metabolism may slow down, your hair might take on more silver hues, and sadly, you may experience more losses — whether it's relationships that no longer serve you or the heartache of losing loved ones. But whether you view these changes as positive or negative, joyful or painful, one thing remains true: Change is inevitable. It's a sign that you're alive, growing, and evolving. Just as an egg transforms into a caterpillar, then wraps itself in a chrysalis to emerge as a butterfly, we too transform as we go through this beautiful cycle of life. We are living, breathing organisms constantly evolving into new versions of ourselves.

That's why loving who you are is a vital part of staying WILD. Embrace your wild self with all the wrinkles, worries, and wisdom that come with time. Aging is not just about enduring the passage of time — it's about honoring the incredible journey that has shaped who you are today and who you are still becoming. Every line on your face, every silver strand, every life lesson is a testament to your resilience, growth, and capacity to love.

So as you continue to evolve, remember to offer yourself the same love and compassion you so freely give to others. Celebrate the changes, cherish the memories, and keep loving yourself fiercely — no matter what stage of life you're in.

Drive It Home

As we reach the final stretch of this journey, it's essential to remember that personal growth and reinvention are not one-time events but ongoing processes. Life is dynamic, and so are we. Just as you wouldn't drive a car without seeing to routine maintenance, you shouldn't navigate life without periodically refreshing and resetting your approach. The seven steps to FREEDOM you've encountered in this book are more than just tools — they're a roadmap for continuous evolution, guiding you toward becoming the best version of yourself, over and over again.

In this section, we're going to *drive it home* by reinforcing the importance of revisiting and repeating these steps throughout your life. Each time you circle back, you'll find yourself growing, transforming, and thriving in ways you might not have thought possible. Here's a quick recap of the seven steps to FREEDOM, designed to keep you on course and ensure you're always moving forward, no matter where you are on your journey.

Step 1: Free Yourself

As you continue on your journey to freedom, it's essential to keep the momentum going by regularly revisiting the tools and techniques from the first step. Start by periodically checking in with yourself using the Wheel of Midlife. This simple yet powerful tool helps you assess where you stand in the eight key areas of your life: Family, Finance, Health, Career, Friends, Love, Leisure, and Growth. By doing this regularly, you can identify where you might be feeling stuck or where you need to focus more attention, ensuring your life stays balanced and fulfilling.

Next, never let your inner superhero go dormant. Revisit the Superhero Guide to remind yourself of the unique gifts, strengths, and passions that make you who you are. Keeping these superpowers and superboosters fired up in your daily life will help you maintain a sense of purpose and joy as you move forward.

Last, remember that your mind is either your greatest ally or your biggest obstacle. Make it your best friend by consistently applying the Stop, Drop, and Roll method to catch and transform negative thoughts. Coupled with regular meditation, this practice will help you build new, empowering beliefs that support your ongoing evolution. Listen to the FREEDOM Meditations often to reinforce these changes and keep your mindset strong and positive as you continue to grow and thrive.

Step 2: Reset Your Life

As you continue on your journey of self-discovery and transformation, it's crucial to regularly reset and recalibrate your life. This step is all about shedding the old, embracing the new, and staying aligned with the best version of yourself as you evolve.

Begin by revisiting the Design the New You exercise whenever you feel the need to reimagine or refine your vision of the future. This powerful journaling practice allows you to step into the shoes of your best self, helping you embody the qualities and experiences you desire before they fully manifest. By doing this regularly, you'll stay inspired and motivated to grow as you navigate life's seasons.

Next, pay close attention to your emotions, especially during challenging times. Emotions can be powerful indicators of where you are in your journey, and by using the ACE method — *awareness, choice, engagement* — you can elevate your emotional state, raise your consciousness, and maintain your well-being. This practice will empower you to own your emotions rather than letting them control you, keeping you grounded and focused on your path.

As if doing a spring cleaning of your soul, periodically revisit your life and carve away anything that no longer serves you. Engage in the Statue of You journaling exercise to assess what's helping or hindering your growth. By regularly lightening your emotional load, you free yourself to fully step into your new-and-improved self.

Finally, remember that every experience in life, whether positive or negative, offers you a choice in how you perceive and respond to it. When you encounter difficult times, repeat the Lotus Effect exercise to transform crises into opportunities for awakening. This four-step subconscious release technique will help you shift from merely surviving midlife to truly thriving, allowing you to blossom into the person you're meant to be.

Step 3: Envision a New Future

As you journey through midlife and beyond, it's essential to continually envision the future you desire so you can create it. This step is about dreaming big and then turning those dreams into reality by setting clear intentions and taking action.

Begin by regularly engaging in the Envision a New Future meditation. This exercise allows you to tap into your deepest desires, helping you to envision and feel your ideal life. The more you connect with this vision, the more you align your energy with the life you're meant to live. Make it a yearly tradition to update the Midlife Masterpiece vision board you created in this step, ensuring it reflects your current dreams and aspirations. This practice keeps your goals fresh and motivates you to continually up-level your life.

Next, don't forget that your mind isn't the only thing guiding you toward your dreams — your body plays a crucial role too. As you age, staying mindful of how you care for your body becomes increasingly important. The ABC's of health — *awareness*, *basics*, and *conditioning* — serve as a simple yet powerful guide to maintaining your physical well-being. Regularly check in with your body, nourish it with healthy foods, stay active, and practice self-love. Your future self will thank you for the care you take today.

By consistently revisiting these practices, you'll not only keep your dreams alive but also ensure that your mind and body are fully equipped to bring those dreams to life. Remember, your future is a blank canvas — paint it with bold strokes, vivid colors, and a vision that excites and inspires you.

Step 4: Embrace and Explore

As you continue to embrace the changes in your life, remember that big dreams don't always require massive leaps — sometimes the small, consistent actions lead to the most significant transformations. Revisit the Quantum Leap method regularly to identify those subtle yet powerful shifts in your daily habits that can propel you toward your newly inspired dreams. By making these small, intentional changes, and holding yourself accountable, you set the stage for quantum leaps in your personal and professional life.

In this process of transformation, mistakes are inevitable, but they are also invaluable. Life isn't about avoiding mistakes — it's about learning from them. As you move forward, keep the My Mistakes Roadmap handy, not as a record of failures, but as a testament to your growth. Each mistake is an opportunity to reset, regroup, and refine your approach. And remember, it's perfectly okay to pivot when necessary. This mindset will not only boost your confidence but also keep you on the path to healing, learning, and continuous progress. By embracing this approach, you empower yourself to explore new possibilities without fear, knowing that every step forward — even the missteps — are part of your journey to becoming the best version of yourself.

Step 5: Detach from Tomorrow

This step is all about letting go of rigid plans and embracing the beauty of spontaneity and the present moment. Life has a way of surprising us when we leave space for the unexpected, so don't be afraid to stray from your usual routine. Regularly tap into the Spontaneity Spark method — a playful approach that includes tools like the Spontaneity Jar — to help you break free from the constraints of overplanning. By doing so, you invite new energy, creativity, and excitement into your life, enriching your journey with the joys of spontaneity and the discovery of new passions.

Additionally, as you navigate midlife, you'll inevitably encounter situations and people that challenge your sense of control. Remember to repeat the Trigger to Treasure technique whenever you feel triggered. This method helps you transform moments of frustration into opportunities for growth and freedom. By embracing positive affirmations, accepting what you cannot change, and using meditation to disconnect from negative energy, you'll find that letting go of control brings a profound sense of peace and liberation. These practices will keep you grounded in the present, allowing you to live each day fully and freely.

Step 6: Own Your Badass Self

As you continue to evolve and step into your power, it's crucial to protect the new version of yourself by setting and maintaining healthy boundaries. Remember, as your internal world shifts, so too will your external relationships. Some people may struggle with the changes you're making, but that's all the more reason to stay true to yourself. Revisit the Four D's of Setting Healthy Boundaries regularly to reinforce your self-esteem, self-worth, and self-acceptance. This process will help you *define*, *decide*, *declare*, and *dedicate yourself* to maintaining strong boundaries that protect the warrior within.

By staying committed to these practices, you'll continue to own your badass self, living confidently and authentically in every area of your life.

Step 7: Master Yourself

Mastering yourself is about developing the resilience to bounce back quickly when life inevitably throws you a curveball. We all face tough times, but the key is not letting those bad moments spiral into prolonged funks that can drain your energy and joy. Regularly revisit the nine tools from the "Unfunk Yourself" chapter whenever you feel yourself slipping into negativity. One powerful example is the 3-2-1 Grounding technique, which helps you reset by anchoring your awareness in the present moment using your senses. These tools are designed to help you overcome a bad day swiftly, allowing you to return to living your best midlife with strength, clarity, and positivity.

As you continue on your journey, remember to Stay WILD: *wake up with gratitude*, *invite more miracles into your life*, *love who you are*, and *drive it home* by living each day to its fullest. Life is short, and mastering yourself means making the most of every moment, squeezing as much joy, fun, and love as you can into your time here. By staying WILD, you give yourself the strength to navigate the hard days and the presence to truly savor the good ones — so no matter what life brings, you're living with intention, resilience, and heart. Revisit the *Dear Me* Letter (the final exercise you're about to undertake) whenever you need a reset, a reminder, or a reflection of how far you've come — and who you're still becoming.

Remember, this journey of self-discovery and transformation is ongoing. By repeating these steps throughout your life, you ensure that you're always moving forward, always growing, and always stepping into your next, most extraordinary self.

 *Dear Me* Letter: A Celebration of Your Growth

As you wrap up this transformative journey and reflect on the tools you've embraced, it's important to acknowledge your progress. You've laid the groundwork to bring your dream life into existence, but the journey doesn't stop here. A year from now, you'll look back on today and be amazed by how far you've come.

To help solidify the changes you've made and manifest your desired future achievements, take a moment to write a *Dear Me* letter. Imagine it's one year from now, and everything in that year has gone as well as you could have hoped. Let your future self reflect on everything you've accomplished over the past year, the boundaries you've set, the gratitude you've felt, and the personal growth you've experienced.

In this letter, your future self will offer words of encouragement, pride, and wisdom, reminding you of the incredible potential you've unlocked. Use the following prompts to guide your letter:

- I'm so proud of you for embracing your journey of self-discovery and transformation. Over the past year, you've...
- The boundaries you've set have helped you...
- You've learned to wake up with gratitude and invite more miracles into your life, which has brought...
- You've faced challenges, but you've handled them with grace and strength by...
- The new experiences you've embraced have taught you...
- As you continue to grow and evolve, I encourage you to keep...

Take your time with this exercise and allow your future self's voice to guide you. This letter will serve as a beautiful reminder of the journey you're on and the future you're building — one step at a time.

The "End"

This may be the end of our journey together in these pages, but it's just the beginning of yours. As you step forward, know that the path ahead is full of possibilities, growth, and endless opportunities to evolve. Your story is still unfolding, and the best is yet to come. Embrace the adventure with open arms, a wild heart, and the courage to live fully, love deeply, and thrive through this thing called life.

I look forward to the day when I meet you in that long line of my dreams, awaiting your copy of *Women Waking Up*. And when I sign it, I'll write:

I knew you could do it!
XO,
Wendy Valentine

ACKNOWLEDGMENTS

Dear universe,

You never cease to amaze me. Seriously, how did you manage to orchestrate all the right people, in all the right places, at exactly the right moments to make this dream come to life? You really outdid yourself this time! A special shout-out to all the stars you lined up so perfectly along my path:

Mom and Dad: You absolutely get the #1 thank-you! Not just for raising this wild child, but for being the ultimate example of how to grab life by the balls and go all in. Mom, your boundless energy paired with Dad's unstoppable perseverance? Yeah, that's the magic combo that made this all possible.

Bryan: Dude, remember that time we went clubbin' in Little Rock, Arkansas, and tore up the dance floor to Beastie Boys' "Intergalactic"? You better believe we're doing that all over again when I meet you in heaven! Thank you for being the best bro ever.

Alexander, Nicholas, Nolan: You know you're something seriously special when the book is dedicated to you *and* you get a shout-out in the acknowledgments. I may have brought you into this world, but let's be real — you're the ones who gave life to me. Thank you for always cheering for your mom and for being such incredible men in the world.

Aunt Annie: If I ever need a good laugh, all I have to do is picture your lil' legs sprinting through that Paris train station! Thank you for always being by my side on this wild roller coaster of life and for patiently listening to me whine for hundreds of hours. And by the way, I finally took your advice: I pulled up my bootstraps and made it happen!

Alex: My twin flame, Daisy's dad, and ultimate partner in crime — thank you for embracing life's adventures with me. Whether we're trekking to Coronado Island on a rickshaw, drinking *ponchas* with our fur baby in Madeira, or belting out karaoke at an RV park, you make life a blissful journey. Thank you for feeding my soul and helping bring this book into the world.

Baka Lily: Thank you for making me delicious Serbian soup and crocheting the cutest little booties while I worked away on my laptop. Your sweet morning kisses on my forehead and calling me "Shakespeare" always lifted my spirits. I truly admire your strength and the love you show for family.

Amy: From that glorious moment twenty-eight years ago, when you waddled your pregnant self into Paradise Valley Mall and let out a fart, I knew we were destined to be best friends for life. That set the stage for sipping 'tinis in Scottsdale, dancing our hearts out in Vegas, and literally peeing our pants in Santa Monica. Thank you for being such an extraordinary woman in my life.

Kae: Girrrrl, you're like my own little Buddha. I'm so grateful our paths crossed in spinning class, and that we've kept moving forward together, trusting the unknown and enjoying spicy margaritas along the way. I'm beyond thankful for you, Gary, and of course, Tito's Teddy. Your love is woven throughout every page of this book.

Kristina Sundermann: How are my plants doing? I hope they're thriving — because thanks to you, I'm growing too. It was no coincidence that I found you when I needed you most. This book is a testament to the love, care, and wisdom you so graciously offer your clients. Of all the voices in my head, yours is by far the best one.

Stefanie Gass: Thank you for being my lighthouse, always guiding me toward my true purpose and leading me straight to Ale. You are, without a doubt, my podcast superhero.

Ale Merino: You turned my business into a beautiful masterpiece — thank you for your amazing vision. What are we creating next?

Lisa Kathan: In a sea of photographers, I found the best one! Thank you for capturing all the many facets of Wendy.

Jack Rose: From building houses to building podcasts, I couldn't be more grateful to have you by my side on this journey. Your support has been invaluable every step of the way.

Michele Martin: Just like ABBA, I was hoping you'd take a chance on me — and you did! The universe lined me up with the best agent I could have dreamed of. Thank you for going to bat for me and helping *Women Waking Up* come to life and reach the world.

Amy B. Scher: Who would've thought that reading your incredible books would change my life, and then someday you'd become my book coach and change my life all over again? No coincidence there! You're not only a brilliant writer and an amazing coach, but also a truly beautiful soul. I can't wait to hug you and thank you in person! Drinks on me!

New World Library: For a first-time author, you've made this entire journey feel seamless and extra special from the very beginning. From the creation of the stunning book cover to Georgia Hughes's exceptional editing, it's clear this book is set to be a worldwide success. Thank you for being the catalyst that turned my dreams into reality.

My podcast peeps: A huge thank-you to all the amazing listeners and gracious guests of *The Midlife Makeover Show*. Your love and loyalty have elevated the podcast into what it is today, and in turn, created the opportunity for this book to be born. Let's keep this midlife party rolling, shall we?

NOTES

Chapter 3: Become Your Own BFF

p. 50 *made up of 99.99999 percent energy:* Joe Dispenza, *Breaking the Habit of Being Yourself: How to Lose Your Mind and Create a New One* (Hay House, 2012), xx.

p. 50 *Here are some key advantages:* Matthew Thorpe and Rachael Ajmera, "How Meditation Benefits Your Mind and Body," *Healthline,* last updated August 15, 2024, https://www.healthline.com/nutrition/12-benefits-of-meditation; Jeremy Sutton, "20+ Health Benefits of Meditation According to Science," *Positive Psychology,* June 19, 2019, https://positivepsychology.com/benefits-of-meditation; "What Meditation Can Do for Your Mind, Mood, and Health," *Harvard Health Publishing,* July 16, 2014, https://www.health.harvard.edu/staying-healthy/what-meditation-can-do-for-your-mind-mood-and-health-; "10 Health Benefits of Meditation and How to Focus on Mindfulness," *UC Davis Health,* December 14, 2022, https://health.ucdavis.edu/blog/cultivating-health/10-health-benefits-of-meditation-and-how-to-focus-on-mindfulness-and-compassion/2022/12.

Chapter 4: Step into the New You

p. 55 *Big Hairy Audacious Goal, a term coined by Jim Collins and Jerry I. Porras:* James C. Collins and Jerry I. Porras, *Built to Last: Successful Habits of Visionary Companies* (Harper Business, 2004; repr., 2002), 9.

Chapter 7: Choose to Be Awakened

p. 79 *"You have the freedom to be yourself, your true self":* Richard Bach, *Jonathan Livingston Seagull: The Complete Edition* (1970; repr., Scribner, 2014), 80.

p. 80 *"Overcome space, and all we have left is Here":* Bach, *Jonathan Livingston Seagull,* 61.

Chapter 9: Love the Body You Live In

p. 106 *On average, women spend an astonishing seventeen years:* "Average Woman Spends 17 Years of Her Life on Diets," *Medical Daily*, September 18, 2012, https://www.medicaldaily.com/average-woman-spends-17-years-her-life-diets-242601.

p. 106 *the average lifespan of a woman in the United States is 80.2 years:* Centers for Disease Control and Prevention, National Center for Health Statistics, "Life Expectancy," October 25, 2024, https://www.cdc.gov/nchs/fastats/life-expectancy.htm.

p. 106 *Annually, Americans spend over $90 billion on dieting and weight loss:* John LaRosa, "U.S. Weight Loss Industry Grows to $90 Billion, Fueled by Obesity Drugs Demand," *Market Research Blog*, March 6, 2024, https://blog.marketresearch.com/u.s.-weight-loss-industry-grows-to-90-billion-fueled-by-obesity-drugs-demand.

p. 106 *women spent around $16.5 billion in 2018 on cosmetic plastic surgery:* "Americans Spent More Than $16.5 Billion on Cosmetic Plastic Surgery in 2018," American Society of Plastic Surgeons, April 10, 2019, https://www.plasticsurgery.org/news/press-releases/americans-spent-more-than-16-billion-on-cosmetic-plastic-surgery-in-2018.

p. 107 *40 percent of women reported feeling anxious:* "Body Image in Adulthood," Mental Health Foundation, accessed April 25, 2025, https://www.mentalhealth.org.uk/our-work/research/body-image-how-we-think-and-feel-about-our-bodies/body-image-adulthood.

p. 115 *"The world's longest-lived people don't pump iron":* Dan Buettner, "Power 9: Reverse Engineering Longevity," Blue Zones, November 2016, https://www.bluezones.com/2016/11/power-9/.

p. 115 *Recent studies show that as little as ten minutes of walking:* Public Health England, "10 Minutes Brisk Walking Each Day in Mid-life for Health Benefits and Towards Achieving Physical Activity Recommendations: Evidence Summary," August 2017, https://assets.publishing.service.gov.uk/government/uploads/system/uploads/attachment_data/file/639030/Health_benefits_of_10_mins_brisk_walking_evidence_summary.pdf.

p. 116 *Reduced hot flashes and night sweats:* Ruta Nonacs, "Why Exercise Helps with Menopausal Hot Flashes," MGH Center for Women's Mental Health, February 1, 2017, https://womensmentalhealth.org/posts/in-brief-why-exercise-helps-with-menopausal-hot-flashes.

p. 116 *Improved mood and reduced anxiety:* "The Role of Exercise in Managing Menopause Symptoms," Australian Menopause Centre, December 5, 2023, https://www.menopausecentre.com.au/the-role-of-exercise-in-managing-menopause-symptoms/.

p. 116 *Better sleep:* "The Role of Exercise in Managing Menopause Symptoms,"

Australian Menopause Centre; Lisa Wartenberg, "Diet and Fitness Tips for Menopause: An Essential Guide," *Healthline*, last reviewed October 14, 2024, https://www.healthline.com/nutrition/menopause-nutrition-fitness-tips#bottom-line.

p. 117 *Weight management:* Jennifer M. Payne, "Why You Should Exercise Your Way Through Menopause," *Lancaster General Health*, February 18, 2021, https://www.lancastergeneralhealth.org/health-hub-home/2021/february/why-you-should-exercise-your-way-through-menopause.

p. 117 *Stronger bones:* Jennifer M. Payne, "Why You Should Exercise Your Way Through Menopause," *Lancaster General Health*; Kim Grundy, "6 Best Exercises for Menopause Symptoms," *GoodRx*, March 13, 2024, https://www.goodrx.com/conditions/menopause/best-exercises-for-menopause.

p. 117 *Higher energy levels:* "The Role of Exercise in Managing Menopause Symptoms," Australian Menopause Centre.

p. 117 *Improved cardiovascular health:* Lisa Wartenberg, "Diet and Fitness Tips for Menopause: An Essential Guide," *Healthline*; Kim Grundy, "6 Best Exercises for Menopause Symptoms," *GoodRx*.

p. 117 *Enhanced cognitive function:* Jennifer M. Payne, "Why You Should Exercise Your Way Through Menopause," *Lancaster General Health*.

p. 117 *Reduced joint pain and stiffness:* "The Role of Exercise in Managing Menopause Symptoms," Australian Menopause Centre; Kim Grundy, "6 Best Exercises for Menopause Symptoms," *GoodRx*.

p. 117 *Increased libido and sexual health:* HPH Editorial Team, "How to Increase Sex Drive During Menopause," *Hot Pause Health*, July 10, 2024, https://hotpausehealth.com/how-to-increase-sex-drive-during-menopause/.

Chapter 11: Embrace Mistakes

p. 133 *"Our deepest fear is not that we are inadequate":* Marianne Williamson, *A Return to Love: Reflections on the Principles of A Course in Miracles* (HarperCollins, 1992), 165.

Chapter 14: Set Healthy Boundaries

p. 185 *While divorce rates have declined among younger adults:* Kerry Law, "The Rise of Grey Divorce: 'It Was Hell After 40 Years of Marriage — but Now I'm Loving Life,'" *Woman & Home*, March 29, 2025, https://www.womanandhome.com/health-wellbeing/grey-divorce/.

p. 186 *"I wish I'd had the courage to live a life true to myself":* Bronnie Ware, *The Top Five Regrets of the Dying: A Life Transformed by the Dearly Departing* (Hay House, 2019), 44.

Chapter 15: Unfunk Yourself

p. 212 *Exercise has been shown to improve mood:* Andreas Heissel et al., "Exercise as Medicine for Depressive Symptoms?: A Systematic Review and Meta-Analysis with Meta-Regression," *British Journal of Sports Medicine* 57, no. 16 (August 2023): 1049–57, https://bjsm.bmj.com/content/bjsports/early/2023/02/14/bjsports-2022-106282.full.pdf.

p. 214 *Studies have shown that forest bathing:* Ye Wen, Qi Yan, Yangliu Pan, Xinren Gu, and Yuanqiu Liu, "Medical Empirical Research on Forest Bathing (*Shinrin-yoku*): A Systematic Review," *Environmental Health and Preventive Medicine* 24, no. 70 (2019), https://doi.org/10.1186/s12199-019-0822-8.

ABOUT THE AUTHOR

Wendy Valentine is a speaker, certified professional life coach, and author of *Women Waking Up* — a midlife rebel on a mission to help women reignite their spark and embrace the magic of midlife.

As the host of *The Midlife Makeover Show* podcast, ranked in the top 1 percent globally and #1 in midlife on iTunes and Spotify, Wendy inspires her listeners to embrace the magic of midlife and live with passion and purpose. Through her transformative group coaching program, FREEDOM at Midlife, and her in-person retreats, Wendy helps women kick fear to the curb, reclaim their joy, and live life on their terms.

Whether she's soaking up the beauty of Madeira, Portugal, or cruising across the USA in her trusty motorhome, Felisha, Wendy lives for adventure and believes that life only gets better with age. Join her on this wild ride by following her on Instagram @wendy_valentine_ and learn more about her journey at WendyValentine.com.

NEW WORLD LIBRARY is dedicated to publishing books and other media [illegible] to improve the quality of our lives and the world.

[illegible] environmentally [illegible] and [illegible]

[illegible]

[illegible] New World Library [illegible]

[illegible]

Our products are available wherever books are [illegible]

[illegible] www.newworldlibrary.com

[illegible]

NEW WORLD LIBRARY is dedicated to publishing books and other media that inspire and challenge us to improve the quality of our lives and the world.

We are a socially and environmentally aware company. We recognize that we have an ethical responsibility to our readers, our authors, our staff members, and our planet.

We serve our readers by creating the finest publications possible on personal growth, creativity, spirituality, wellness, and other areas of emerging importance. We serve our authors by working with them to produce and promote quality books that reach a wide audience. We serve New World Library employees with generous benefits, significant profit sharing, and constant encouragement to pursue their most expansive dreams.

We print our books with soy-based ink on paper from sustainably managed forests. We power our Northern California office with solar energy, and we respectfully acknowledge that it is located on the ancestral lands of the Coast Miwok Indians. We also contribute to nonprofit organizations working to make the world a better place for us all.

Our products are available wherever books are sold.

customerservice@NewWorldLibrary.com
Phone: 415-884-2100 or 800-972-6657
Orders: Ext. 110
Fax: 415-884-2199
NewWorldLibrary.com

Scan below to access our newsletter
and learn more about our books and authors.